Louis Weber, CEO
Publications International, Ltd.
8140 Lehigh Ave
Morton Grove, IL 60053

Pictured on the front cover: Sausage Spaghetti *(page 142).*

Pictured on the back cover *(left to right):* Pepperoni Pizza Puffs *(page 22)* and Ice Cream Cone Cupcakes *(page 148).*

ISBN: 978-1-64030-149-8

Manufactured in China.

8 7 6 5 4 3 2 1

Microwave Cooking: Microwave ovens vary in wattage. Use the cooking times as guidelines and check for doneness before adding more time.

COOKING
HACKS

TIPS AND TRICKS TO MAKE COOKING FASTER, EASIER AND MORE FUN, WITH MORE THAN 70 RECIPES

Publications International, Ltd.

TABLE OF CONTENTS

INGREDIENT HACKS

BISCUIT DOUGH

Mini Biscuit Doughnuts 6
Quick Jelly-Filled Biscuit Doughnuts . . 8
Cookie Dough Monkey Bread 10
Super Simple Cheesy Bubble Loaf. . .12
Cinnamon-Sugar Twists. 14

RAMEN NOODLES

Ramen Egg Cups 16
Ramen Bites on a Stick 18
Ramen French Toast. 20
Pepperoni Pizza Puffs 22
Tahini Lentil Ramen Salad. 24

CAKE MIX

PB & J Sandwich Cake. 26
Peach Strawberry Dump Cake. 28
Mixed Berry Dump Cake 30
Rainbow Cake 32
Minty Cookies and Cream Cake. . . . 34

PIZZA DOUGH

Breakfast Flats. 36
Pepperoni Pizza Rolls. 38
Sausage and Kale
Deep-Dish Mini Pizzas 40

BACON

Bacon and Egg Cups 42
Caramelized Bacon. 44
Chocolate-Covered Bacon 46

EGGS

Ham and Asparagus Quiche. 48
Cheddar, Broccoli and
Mushroom Quiche. 50
Bacon and Egg Wraps. 52
Easy Eggs Benedict 54
Egg Salad Sandwiches. 56
Curried Deviled Eggs 58

BANANAS

Chocolate Chip-Banana
Muffin Bars 60
Spiced Banana Bread. 62
Banana Chocolate-Chunk
Cupcakes. 64
Ripe Banana Muffins. 66
Spiced Maple Banana
Oatmeal Smoothie 68
Banana Split Shakes. 70
Breakfast Banana Split Smoothie. . . 70

PUMPKIN

Pumpkin and Parmesan
Twice-Baked Potatoes. 72
Pumpkin Ravioli. 74
Pumpkin Curry. 76
Pumpkin Spice Latte 78
Pumpkin Mac and Cheese. 80

APPLIANCE AND PAN HACKS

WAFFLE MAKER

Cheesy Mashed Potato Waffles.... 82
Waffled Burger Sliders............ 84
Quick Waffled Quesadillas 86
Waffled Panko Mac and Cheese ... 88

SLOW COOKER

Blueberry-Orange
French Toast Casserole 90
Steamed Pork Buns 92
Italian Cheesecake 94
Focaccia with
Rosemary and Romano........... 96
No-Fuss Macaroni and Cheese 98
Pepperoni Pizza Monkey Bread... 100

MUFFIN TIN

Mac and Cheese Mini Cups....... 102
Pumpkin Tartlets................ 104
Mini Fruit Coffeecakes........... 106
Quick and Easy Arancini 108
Chocolate Chip Cookie Delights ... 110
Tortilla Cups with
Corn and Black Bean Salad 112

BUNDT PAN

Corn Fritters.................... 114
Chili Corn Bread 116
Corn Chowder 118
Easy Cheesy Bacon Bread 120
Huevos Ramencheros 122

MISCELLANEOUS HACKS

ICE CREAM SCOOP

Buttermilk Drop Biscuits..........124
Cream Cheese Cupcakes..........126
Sweet and Savory
Breakfast Muffins.................128

LEFTOVERS

Leftover Candy Cupcakes
with Peanut Butter Frosting...... 130
Cake Bonbons 132
Italian Crouton Salad 134
Tropical Turkey Salad.............136
Leftover Candy Ice Cream Sundae
with Hard Chocolate Topping 138

KID STUFF

Not-So-Sloppy Joes............. 140
Sausage Spaghetti 142
Meat Loaf Cupcakes............ 144
Wild Watermelon Pops 146
Ice Cream Cone Cupcakes 148
Cookie Sundae Cups 150
Broccoli Surprise
Corn Muffins....................152

BISCUIT DOUGH

MINI BISCUIT DOUGHNUTS

MAKES 10 DOUGHNUTS

> Vegetable oil for frying
> 1 package (7½ ounces) refrigerated biscuits (10 biscuits)
> Honey and chopped pistachios

1 Pour about 2 inches of oil into Dutch oven or large heavy saucepan; clip deep-fry or candy thermometer to side of pot. Heat over medium-high heat to 360° to 370°F. Line wire rack with paper towels.

2 Meanwhile, poke holes in biscuits with handle of wooden spoon or tip of funnel. Cook biscuits about 1½ minutes or until golden brown, turning once. Drain on prepared wire rack. Drizzle with honey and sprinkle with pistachios. Serve warm.

CHOCOLATE VARIATION

For chocolate glaze, heat ¼ cup whipping cream in small saucepan over medium heat until bubbles appear around edge of pan. Stir in ½ cup semisweet chocolate chips until melted and smooth. Dip tops of doughnuts in glaze; decorate with sprinkles, if desired.

HACKED!

Frying biscuit dough is the quickest way to hot homemade doughnuts. This recipe is amazingly simple, but with only a bit more effort you can have jelly doughnuts (page 8) or cinnamon-sugar twists (page 14).

QUICK JELLY-FILLED BISCUIT DOUGHNUTS

MAKES 10 DOUGHNUTS

Vegetable oil for frying

⅓ cup granulated sugar or coarse decorating sugar

1 package (7½ ounces) refrigerated biscuits (10 biscuits)

1 cup strawberry preserves*

If preserves are very chunky, process in food processor 10 seconds or press through fine-mesh sieve.

1 Pour about 2 inches of oil into Dutch oven or large heavy saucepan; clip deep-fry or candy thermometer to side of pot. Heat over medium-high heat to 360°F to 370°F. Line wire rack with paper towels.

2 Place sugar in medium bowl. Separate biscuits. Fry in batches 1 minute per side until puffed and golden. Drain briefly on prepared rack; while still warm, toss in sugar to coat.

3 Fit piping bag with medium star tip; fill bag with preserves. Poke hole in side of each doughnut with paring knife; fill with preserves. Serve immediately.

HACKED!

If you don't have a piping bag or pastry tips, you can use a squeeze bottle instead. Generally a food storage bag with a corner snipped of can substitute for a piping bag and tip, but to really force the preserves into these doughnuts you'll need something with a tip.

COOKIE DOUGH MONKEY BREAD
MAKES 16 SERVINGS

> 1 package (about 16 ounces) break-apart refrigerated chocolate chip cookie dough (24 cookies)
> 2 packages (7½ ounces each) refrigerated buttermilk biscuits (10 biscuits per package)
> 1 cup semisweet chocolate chips, divided
> ¼ cup whipping cream

1 Preheat oven to 350°F. Generously spray 12-cup (10-inch) bundt pan with nonstick cooking spray.

2 Break cookie dough into 24 pieces; split each piece in half to create total of 48 pieces. Separate biscuits; cut each biscuit into four pieces with scissors. Layer half of cookie dough and half of biscuit pieces in prepared pan, alternating doughs. Sprinkle with ¼ cup chocolate chips. Repeat layers with remaining cookie dough and biscuit pieces; sprinkle with ¼ cup chocolate chips.

3 Bake 27 to 30 minutes or until biscuits are golden brown, covering loosely with foil during last 10 minutes of baking. Remove pan to wire rack; let stand, covered, 5 minutes. Loosen edges of bread with knife; invert onto serving plate.

4 Pour cream into medium microwavable bowl; microwave on HIGH 1 minute or until boiling. Add remaining ½ cup chocolate chips; stir until chocolate is melted. Let stand 5 minutes to thicken slightly. Drizzle glaze over bread.

HACKED!

Biscuit dough and prepared cookie dough come together in this recipe to make a match made in decadent, gooey dessert heaven!

SUPER SIMPLE CHEESY BUBBLE LOAF

MAKES 12 SERVINGS

> 2 packages (7½ ounces each) refrigerated buttermilk biscuits (10 biscuits per package)
> 2 tablespoons butter, melted
> 1½ cups (6 ounces) shredded Italian cheese blend

1 Preheat oven to 350°F. Spray 9×5-inch loaf pan with nonstick cooking spray.

2 Separate biscuits; cut each biscuit into four pieces with scissors. Layer half of biscuit pieces in prepared pan. Drizzle with 1 tablespoon butter; sprinkle with 1 cup cheese. Top with remaining biscuit pieces, 1 tablespoon butter and ½ cup cheese.

3 Bake about 25 minutes or until golden brown. Serve warm.

HACKED!

This incredibly easy pull-apart bread can be customized in several delicious ways. It's easy to change up the flavors in this simple bread. Try Mexican cheese blend instead of Italian, and add taco seasoning and/or hot pepper sauce to the melted butter before drizzling it over the dough. Or, sprinkle ¼ cup chopped ham, salami or crumbled crisp-cooked bacon between the layers of dough.

CINNAMON-SUGAR TWISTS

MAKES 14 TWISTS

- 1 package (about 8 ounces) crescent dough sheet
- ½ cup sugar
- 1 teaspoon ground cinnamon

1 Heat 2 inches of oil in large saucepan or Dutch oven to 360°F.

2 Meanwhile, unroll dough on work surface. Cut crosswise into 1-inch strips. Roll strips to form thin ropes; fold in half and twist halves together. Combine sugar and cinnamon in baking dish or shallow bowl.

3 Fry twists about 1½ minutes or until golden brown, turning once. Drain on paper towel-lined wire rack 2 minutes; roll in cinnamon-sugar to coat. Serve warm.

HACKED!

Although these twists are made with crescent dough, they deserve a place in this chapter alongside biscuit dough. If you can't find crescent dough sheets, buy regular crescent rolls, unroll them onto a lightly floured surface and press the seams together. Proceed with step 2.

RAMEN NOODLES

RAMEN EGG CUPS

MAKES 6 SERVINGS

> 1 **package (3 ounces) chicken-flavored ramen noodles**
> 6 **eggs**
> 2 **tablespoons milk**
> **Salt and black pepper**
> **Chopped fresh parsley**

1 Preheat oven to 400°F. Crush 6 pieces of foil into balls about half the size of standard (2½-inch) muffin cups. Spray 6 muffin cups and foil balls with nonstick cooking spray.

2 Fill medium saucepan half full with water; add seasoning packet and bring to a boil over high heat. Add noodles; cook 1 minute to soften. Drain and rinse under cold water.

3 Divide noodles among prepared muffin cups, pressing into bottoms and up sides. Place foil ball in each cup to help set shape.

4 Bake 15 minutes. Remove foil balls; return to oven and bake 10 to 12 minutes. Cool in pan 5 minutes. *Reduce oven temperature to 325°F.*

5 Carefully crack 1 egg into each cup. Top each egg with 1 teaspoon milk; season with salt and pepper. Bake 10 to 12 minutes until egg whites are completely set and yolks are thickened but not hard. Top with chopped parsley. Serve warm.

HACKED!

Ramen noodles have so many uses beyond a quick lunch. Here they make a savory, crunchy egg cup.

RAMEN BITES ON A STICK

MAKES 24 BITES

> 4 packages (3 ounces each) ramen noodles, any flavor
> 1 can (12 ounces) evaporated milk
> 2 cups (8 ounces) finely shredded Cheddar cheese
> ¼ teaspoon salt
> ¼ teaspoon garlic powder
> 2 eggs
> 1 cup panko bread crumbs

1 Preheat oven to 350°F. Spray 13×9-inch pan with nonstick cooking spray. Prepare noodles according to package directions (discard seasoning packets). Drain and rinse under cold water to cool completely. Place in medium bowl.

2 Add evaporated milk, cheese, salt and garlic powder; stir to mix well. Spread noodle mixture in prepared pan. Bake 30 minutes. Cool in pan on wire rack 10 minutes. Cover and refrigerate 4 to 6 hours.

3 Preheat oven to 425°F. Spray large baking sheet with cooking spray. Cut noodle mixture into 24 squares.

4 Beat eggs in shallow bowl. Place panko in another shallow bowl. Using fork, dip each ramen square in egg mixture, coating well; roll in panko to coat completely. Place on baking sheet. Bake 8 minutes; turn over, bake 2 minutes. Cool slightly; insert wooden sticks for serving, if desired.

HACKED!

This fun party snack is easy to make ahead and finish just before serving. Breaded noodle squares can be refrigerated for several hours before baking. Make a double batch because they'll go quickly!

RAMEN FRENCH TOAST

MAKES 4 SLICES

 2 eggs
 ½ cup milk
 ¼ cup maple syrup, plus additional for serving
 1 teaspoon ground cinnamon
 2 packages (3 ounces each) ramen noodles, any flavor
 1 tablespoon butter
   Powdered sugar (optional)

1 Whisk eggs, milk, ¼ cup syrup and cinnamon in 13×9-inch glass baking dish until well blended. Carefully break each noodle block into two square pieces of "bread" (discard seasoning packets). Place in egg mixture, turn over to coat well. Let stand 30 minutes to soften, turning once.

2 Heat butter in large skillet over medium heat. Add noodle pieces; cook 3 minutes per side until golden brown. Serve warm with additional syrup or dust with powdered sugar.

HACKED!

You've never seen noodles do this before! In this creative recipe, ramen stands in for bread and gets fried up like French toast.

PEPPERONI PUFFERS
MAKES 24 PIECES

- 1 package (3 ounces) oriental-flavored ramen noodles
- 1 cup (4 ounces) shredded mozzarella cheese
- 2 eggs, beaten
- 1 teaspoon dried Italian seasoning
- ¼ teaspoon red pepper flakes
- ¼ cup prepared pizza sauce
- 2 tablespoons grated Parmesan cheese, plus additional for garnish
- 24 small pepperoni slices (not mini)

1 Preheat oven to 400°F. Spray 24-cup mini muffin pan with nonstick cooking spray.

2 Break noodles into 4 pieces. Cook according to package directions using seasoning packet. Drain well.

3 Combine noodles, mozzarella cheese, eggs, Italian seasoning and red pepper flakes in large bowl.

4 Spoon noodle mixture evenly in each prepared muffin cup. Top each with ½ teaspoon sauce, ¼ teaspoon Parmesan cheese and pepperoni slice.

5 Bake 13 minutes or until centers are firm and noodles are browned around edges. Let stand 10 minutes; remove from pan to wire rack. Sprinkle with additional Parmesan cheese, if desired.

TAHINI LENTIL RAMEN SALAD

MAKES ABOUT 6 CUPS

- 1 cup uncooked brown lentils
- 1 cup small broccoli florets
- 1 package (3 ounces) ramen noodles, any flavor
- 3 tablespoons olive oil
- 1 tablespoon tahini paste
- Juice of 1 lemon
- 1 teaspoon salt
- ⅛ teaspoon red pepper flakes
- 1 medium tomato, diced

1 Bring 6 cups water to boil in medium saucepan over medium-high heat. Add lentils. Reduce heat; cover and simmer 35 minutes. Add broccoli; cook 2 minutes. Add noodles (discard seasoning packet); cook 2 minutes. Drain well.

2 Whisk oil, tahini, lemon juice, salt and red pepper flakes in large bowl until well blended. Add lentil mixture and tomato; toss to coat well. Refrigerate 20 minutes.

HACKED!

This easy one-pot meal can be packed in jars to take for lunches throughout the week. Add a light sprinkling of salt, a drizzle of olive oil and a squeeze of lemon juice just before serving to brighten the flavors.

PB & J SANDWICH CAKE

MAKES 12 SERVINGS

- 1 package (about 15 ounces) white cake mix, plus ingredients to prepare mix
- ¾ cup powdered sugar
- 5 tablespoons peanut butter
- 2 to 3 tablespoons whipping cream or milk
- 1 tablespoon butter, softened
- ½ cup strawberry or grape jam

1 Preheat oven to 350°F. Grease two 8-inch square baking pans. Prepare cake mix according to package directions. Spread batter evenly in prepared pans.

2 Bake 30 minutes or until toothpick inserted into centers comes out clean. Cool cake layers in pans on wire racks 30 minutes. Remove to wire racks; cool completely.

3 Carefully slice off browned tops of both layers to create flat, even layers. Place one layer on serving plate, cut side up.

4 Beat powdered sugar, peanut butter, 2 tablespoons cream and butter in medium bowl with electric mixer at medium speed until light and creamy. Add remaining 1 tablespoon cream, if necessary, to reach spreading consistency. Gently spread filling over cut side of cake layer on serving plate. Spread jam over peanut butter filling. Top with second cake layer, cut side up. Cut cake in half diagonally. To serve, cut into thin slices across the diagonal.

HACKED!

The color and texture of white cake mix looks just like sandwich bread in this fun snack cake. Serve it with potato chips and apple slices to complete the illusion of lunch for dessert!

PEACH STRAWBERRY DUMP CAKE

MAKES 12 TO 16 SERVINGS

  1 can (29 ounces) peach slices in light syrup, undrained

1½ cups frozen sliced strawberries, thawed and drained

  1 package (about 15 ounces) yellow cake mix

  ½ cup (1 stick) butter, melted

    Ice cream (optional)

1 Preheat oven to 350°F. Spray 13×9-inch baking pan with nonstick cooking spray.

2 Spread peaches and strawberries in prepared pan. Top with cake mix, spreading evenly. Pour butter over top, covering cake mix as much as possible.

3 Bake 50 to 55 minutes or until toothpick inserted into center of cake comes out clean. Cool at least 15 minutes before serving. Serve with ice cream, if desired.

HACKED!

Did you know that cake mix makes the easiest cobbler topping for baked fruit? Just spread it over the fruit, top with butter and bake!

MIXED BERRY DUMP CAKE

MAKES 12 TO 16 SERVINGS

2 packages (12 ounces each) frozen mixed berries, thawed and drained

1 package (about 15 ounces) white cake mix

¼ teaspoon ground cinnamon

1 can (12 ounces) lemon-lime soda

½ cup cinnamon chips

1 Preheat oven to 350°F. Spray 13×9-inch baking pan with nonstick cooking spray.

2 Spread berries in prepared pan. Top with cake mix, spreading evenly. Sprinkle with cinnamon. Slowly pour soda over top, covering cake mix as much as possible. Sprinkle with cinnamon chips.

3 Bake 45 to 50 minutes or until toothpick inserted into center of cake comes out clean. Cool at least 15 minutes before serving.

HACKED!

Cake mix and soda work together like magic to create a cakelike topping for frozen fruit in seconds.

RAINBOW CAKE

MAKES 12 TO 15 SERVINGS

1 package (about 15 ounces) white cake mix, plus ingredients to prepare mix

Gel food coloring (6 colors)

1 package (4-serving size) orange gelatin

1 cup boiling water

½ cup cold water

1 container (8 ounces) frozen whipped topping, thawed

½ cup colored nonpareils

1 Prepare cake mix according to package directions. Divide batter evenly into six small bowls. Add one food coloring to each individual bowl until desired shade is reached.

2 Prop one end of 13×9-inch pan on wooden spoon; alternately pour batters in crosswise lines into pan. Bake according to package directions; cool completely.

3 Poke holes in cake at ½-inch intervals with fork. Combine gelatin and boiling water in small bowl; stir until gelatin is dissolved. Stir in cold water. Cool gelatin slightly; pour over cake. Top cake with whipped topping and nonpareils. Refrigerate until ready to serve.

HACKED!

Did you know that cake mix could be this colorful? To achieve the even rainbow stripes, make sure your pan is slightly elevated on one end and pour the batters in stripes on the low end. You could also swirl the batters for a tie-dyed effect or even layer them in muffin pan cups for rainbow cupcakes. And feel free to skip the gelatin in step 3 if you want—it won't affect the colors, just the taste.

MINTY COOKIES AND CREAM CAKE

MAKES 10 TO 12 SERVINGS

- 1 package (about 15 ounces) white cake mix, plus ingredients to prepare mix
- 20 chocolate creme-filled sandwich cookies, crushed
- 1 package (about 3 ounces) instant white chocolate pudding and pie filling mix
- 2 cups milk
- 1 teaspoon mint extract

  Green food coloring
- ¾ cup whipping cream
- 1 cup semisweet chocolate chips

1 Preheat oven to 350°F. Grease and flour two 9-inch round cake pans.

2 Prepare cake mix according to package directions; stir in cookies. Pour batter evenly into prepared pans. Bake 25 minutes or until toothpick inserted into centers comes out clean. Cool completely in pans on wire rack.

3 Loosen cakes from sides and bottoms of pans with knife. Poke holes all over cakes with round wooden spoon handle. Whisk pudding mix, milk, mint extract and food coloring in large bowl 2 minutes. Spread over cakes. Refrigerate 2 hours.

4 Invert one cake onto second cake in pan; turn out stack of cakes onto serving plate.

5 Heat cream in small saucepan until bubbles form around edge of pan. Remove from heat. Add chips; whisk until smooth. Pour over cake; spread evenly over top and sides. Refrigerate 1 hour or until topping is set.

HACKED!

This type of cake, known as a poke cake, turns a regular cake mix cake into a surprising, pudding-filled dessert.

PIZZA DOUGH

BREAKFAST FLATS

MAKES 4 SERVINGS

> 8 slices bacon, diced
> 1 package (14 ounces) refrigerated pizza dough
> 1½ cups (6 ounces) shredded Cheddar cheese
> 4 eggs
>   Kosher salt and black pepper

1 Preheat oven to 400°F. Line two baking sheets with parchment paper.

2 Heat large nonstick skillet over medium-high heat. Add bacon; cook about 8 minutes or until crisp, stirring occasionally. Drain on paper towel-lined plate, reserving 1 tablespoon drippings in skillet.

3 Divide pizza dough into four equal pieces. Roll out on lightly floured surface into 8×4-inch rectangles. Place dough on prepared baking sheets; top each with cheese and bacon. Bake 10 minutes or until crust is golden brown and crisp and cheese is melted.

4 Heat same skillet over medium heat. Add eggs; cook about 5 minutes or until yolks are desired doneness (cover the skillet to speed up cooking and check eggs frequently).

5 Place one egg on each crust; season with salt and pepper. Serve immediately.

HACKED!

Pizza dough makes an appearance at breakfast in this creative take on everyone's favorite trio: bacon, eggs and toast. For super fast and easy eggs, use the technique on page 54 for poaching eggs in the microwave.

PEPPERONI PIZZA ROLLS

MAKES 12 ROLLS

1 loaf (1 pound) frozen pizza dough or white bread dough, thawed according to package directions

½ cup pizza sauce, plus additional sauce for serving

⅓ cup chopped pepperoni or mini pepperoni slices (half of 2½-ounce package)

9 to 10 slices fontina, provolone or provolone-mozzarella blend cheese*

For best results, use thin cheese slices (less than 1 ounce each).

1 Spray 12 standard (2½-inch) muffin pan cups with nonstick cooking spray.

2 Roll out dough on lightly floured surface into 12×10-inch rectangle. Spread ½ cup pizza sauce over dough, leaving ½-inch border on one long side. Sprinkle with pepperoni; top with cheese, cutting slices to fit as necessary. Starting with long side opposite ½-inch border, roll up dough jelly-roll style; pinch seam to seal.

3 Cut crosswise into 1-inch slices; place slices cut sides up in prepared muffin cups. Cover with plastic wrap; let rise in warm place 30 to 40 minutes or until nearly doubled in size. Preheat oven to 350°F.

4 Bake about 25 minutes or until golden brown. Loosen bottom and sides with small spatula or knife; remove to wire rack. Serve warm with additional sauce for dipping, if desired.

HACKED!

To make perfectly even slices for these pizza rolls without measuring, cut the log into 3 equal pieces. Cut each third of dough in half to make 6 pieces. Cut each of the 6 pieces in half again and you'll have 12 even slices.

SAUSAGE AND KALE DEEP-DISH MINI PIZZAS

MAKES 12 PIZZAS

1 tablespoon olive oil

1 spicy Italian sausage (turkey or pork)

⅓ cup finely chopped red onion

2½ cups packed chopped stemmed kale

¼ teaspoon salt

1 loaf (1 pound) frozen pizza dough or white bread dough, thawed according to package directions

¾ cup (3 ounces) shredded Italian blend cheese

¼ cup pizza sauce

1 Preheat oven to 400°F. Spray 12 standard (2½-inch) muffin pan cups with nonstick cooking spray.

2 Heat oil in large skillet over medium-high heat. (If using pork sausage, oil is not needed.) Remove sausage from casing; crumble into skillet. Cook and stir about 5 minutes or until no longer pink. Remove to plate. Add onion to skillet; cook and stir 4 minutes or until softened. Add kale; cook about 10 minutes or until tender, stirring occasionally. Return sausage to skillet with salt; stir until blended. Set aside to cool slightly.

3 Divide dough into 12 pieces. Stretch or roll each piece into 5-inch circle; press into prepared muffin cups. Sprinkle 1 teaspoon cheese into bottom of each cup; spread 1 teaspoon pizza sauce over cheese. Top evenly with kale mixture and remaining cheese.

4 Bake about 16 minutes or until golden brown. Let stand in pan 1 minute; loosen sides with small spatula or knife. Remove to wire rack. Serve warm.

HACKED!

Individual pizzas have never been cuter! Plan on at least two pizzas per serving and heat up some extra sauce for dipping.

BACON AND EGG CUPS
MAKES 12 SERVINGS

- 12 slices bacon, crisp-cooked and cut crosswise into thirds
- 6 eggs
- ½ cup diced red and green bell pepper
- ½ cup (2 ounces) shredded pepper jack or Monterey Jack cheese
- ½ cup half-and-half
- ¼ teaspoon salt
- ¼ teaspoon black pepper

1 Preheat oven to 350°F. Spray 12 standard (2½-inch) muffin cups with nonstick cooking spray.

2 Place 3 bacon slices in each prepared muffin cup, overlapping in bottom. Beat eggs, bell pepper, cheese, half-and-half, salt and black pepper in medium bowl until well blended. Fill each muffin cup with ¼ cup egg mixture.

3 Bake 20 to 25 minutes or until eggs are set in center. Run knife around edge of each cup before removing from pan.

HACKED!

Forget pie crust as a base for mini quiches and try bacon instead! This recipe uses one slice per cup but you could double that and line the whole cup for an extra bacony breakfast.

CARAMELIZED BACON

MAKES 12 SLICES

12 slices (about 12 ounces) applewood-smoked bacon
½ cup packed brown sugar
2 tablespoons water
¼ to ½ teaspoon ground red pepper

1 Preheat oven to 375°F. Line 15×10-inch jelly-roll pan with heavy-duty foil. Spray wire rack with nonstick cooking spray; place in prepared pan.

2 Cut bacon in half crosswise, if desired; arrange in single layer on prepared wire rack. Combine brown sugar, water and ground red pepper in small bowl; mix well. Brush generously over bacon.

3 Bake 20 to 25 minutes or until bacon is well browned. Immediately remove to serving platter; cool completely.

HACKED!

You know you can fry bacon on the stove, but did you know it's even better baked? And it can even be made up to 3 days ahead, making it a perfect option for parties. Store it in the refrigerator between sheets of waxed paper in a resealable food storage bag. Let it stand at room temperature at least 30 minutes before serving.

CHOCOLATE-COVERED BACON
MAKES 12 SLICES

- 12 slices thick-cut bacon
- 12 wooden skewers (12 inches)
- 1 cup semisweet chocolate chips
- 1 cup white chocolate chips or butterscotch chips
- 2 tablespoons shortening, divided

1 Preheat oven to 400°F. Line 15×10-inch jelly-roll pan with heavy-duty foil. Spray wire rack with nonstick cooking spray; place in prepared pan. Thread each bacon slice onto a wooden skewer. Bake 20 to 25 minutes or until crisp. Cool completely.

2 Combine semisweet chocolate chips and 1 tablespoon shortening in large microwavable bowl. Heat on HIGH at 30-second intervals until chocolate is melted and smooth, stirring after each interval.

3 Combine white chocolate chips and remaining 1 tablespoon shortening in large microwavable bowl. Microwave on HIGH at 30-second intervals until melted and smooth, stirring after each interval.

4 Line large baking sheet with waxed or parchment paper. Place bacon on baking sheet. Drizzle both chocolates over bacon. Refrigerate until firm. Store leftovers in refrigerator.

HACKED!

Now that you know all about baking bacon from page 44, use that technique to turn your bacon into dessert! For sweet-salty fans, this is the ultimate treat.

HAM AND ASPARAGUS QUICHE

MAKES 4 TO 6 SERVINGS

2 cups sliced asparagus (½-inch pieces)

1 red bell pepper, chopped

1 cup milk

2 tablespoons all-purpose flour

4 eggs

1 cup chopped cooked deli ham

2 tablespoons chopped fresh basil

½ teaspoon salt

¼ teaspoon black pepper

½ cup (2 ounces) finely shredded Swiss cheese

1 Preheat oven to 350°F. Combine asparagus, bell pepper and 1 tablespoon water in microwavable 9-inch pie plate. Cover with vented plastic wrap; microwave on HIGH 2 minutes or until vegetables are crisp-tender. Drain vegetables.

2 Whisk milk and flour in large bowl. Whisk in eggs until well blended. Stir in vegetables, ham, basil, salt and black pepper. Pour over vegetables in pie plate. Cover with vented plastic wrap.

3 Cook on HIGH about 10 minutes or until eggs are solid all the way through when pierced with knife. Sprinkle with cheese; cover and let stand 2 minutes or until cheese is melted.

HACKED!

This section is all about eggs. Did you know that the microwave can be your best friend when it comes to cooking eggs? Try quiche here and on the next page, or the fastest egg and bacon wrap on page 52. If you haven't used the microwave to poach eggs, you'll be amazed! See page 54 for details. And check out page 56 for tips on cooking perfectly peelable hard-cooked eggs.

CHEDDAR, BROCCOLI AND MUSHROOM QUICHE

MAKES 4 SERVINGS

- 2 teaspoons olive oil
- 6 ounces sliced mushrooms
- 1½ cups small broccoli florets (½-inch pieces)
- 6 eggs *or* 1½ cups egg substitute
- ⅓ cup milk
- ¼ teaspoon dried thyme
- ⅛ teaspoon ground red pepper
- 1 teaspoon salt
- ½ cup finely chopped green onions
- 1 cup (4 ounces) shredded Cheddar cheese, divided

1 Heat oil in large nonstick skillet over medium-high heat. Add mushrooms and broccoli; cook 4 minutes or until mushrooms are soft, stirring frequently. Transfer to 9-inch microwavable pie plate.

2 Whisk eggs, milk, thyme, ground red pepper and salt in medium bowl until well blended. Stir in green onions and ¾ cup cheese. Pour evenly over vegetable mixture. Cover with vented plastic wrap.

3 Cook on HIGH about 10 minutes or until eggs are solid all the way through when pierced with knife. Sprinkle with remaining ¼ cup cheese; cover and let stand 2 minutes or until cheese is melted.

HACKED!

You could bake this quiche, but there's no need when you have a microwave! The microwave makes quick work of eggs, with perfectly fluffy results. For a different flavor combination, try the Ham and Asparagus Quiche on the previous page.

BACON AND EGG WRAPS

MAKES 4 SERVINGS

4 eggs *or* 1 cup egg substitute

¼ cup shredded Parmesan cheese

2 slices Canadian bacon, diced

½ teaspoon hot pepper sauce

¼ teaspoon salt

¼ teaspoon black pepper

4 (7-inch) red chile tortillas or whole wheat tortillas

1 cup baby spinach leaves

1 Spray 9-inch microwavable pie plate with nonstick cooking spray. Whisk eggs, cheese, bacon, hot pepper sauce, salt and black pepper in medium bowl. Pour into prepared pie plate; cover with vented plastic wrap. Microwave on HIGH 3 minutes or until eggs are set.

2 Place tortillas on plate. Microwave 10 seconds or until soft and pliable. Cut egg into quarters. Place one wedge in center of each tortilla. Top with ¼ cup spinach leaves. Fold bottom of tortilla to center; fold sides to center to enclose filling. Serve immediately.

EASY EGGS BENEDICT

MAKES 2 TO 4 SERVINGS

> 2 English muffins, split
> 2 tablespoons butter, softened, divided
> 4 slices Canadian bacon
> 1 cup water
> 1 teaspoon white vinegar
> 8 eggs
> 1 can (6 ounces) hollandaise sauce
>   Dash of ground red pepper

1 Preheat oven to 170°F. Toast English muffin halves; spread with 1 tablespoon butter. Place muffin halves on baking sheet.

2 Place bacon on microwavable plate; microwave on HIGH about 15 seconds or just until warm. Place 1 slice bacon on each muffin half; place in oven to keep warm.

3 Place ¼ cup water and ¼ teaspoon vinegar in each of 4 ramekins or small microwavable bowls. Crack one egg into each ramekin. Cook eggs one at a time for 1 minute on HIGH. Transfer eggs to muffin halves with slotted spoon or fork.

4 Heat hollandaise sauce in small saucepan over low heat or in microwave 1 to 2 minutes or just until warm, stirring frequently. Do not boil. Stir in remaining 2 tablespoons butter and ground red pepper until butter is melted and mixture is smooth and well blended. Spoon warm hollandaise over each egg.

HACKED!

If you think your microwave runs hot, check your eggs at 45 seconds and add more time if needed.

EGG SALAD SANDWICHES
MAKES 4 SERVINGS

6 eggs

½ cup finely chopped celery

¼ cup mayonnaise

1½ tablespoons sweet pickle relish

¼ teaspoon salt

⅛ teaspoon black pepper

8 slices sandwich bread

1 Bring medium saucepan of water to a boil. Gently add eggs with slotted spoon. Reduce heat to maintain a simmer; cook 12 minutes. Meanwhile, prepare ice bath. Drain eggs and place in ice bath; cool 10 minutes.

2 Chop eggs; place in medium bowl. Add celery, mayonnaise, relish, salt and pepper; mix well. Serve on bread.

HACKED!

You've probably heard that the best way to make hard-cooked eggs is to place eggs in cold water, bring to a boil, then cover and steam them off the heat. This way does make perfectly cooked eggs, but they can be hard to peel. When you add eggs to boiling water, you run the risk of cracking the shells and losing a bit of the white but the eggs will be easier to peel.

CURRIED DEVILED EGGS

MAKES 12 SERVINGS

6 eggs

¼ cup mayonnaise

¼ teaspoon curry powder

¼ teaspoon black pepper

⅛ teaspoon salt

Dash of paprika

¼ cup dried sweetened cherries or cranberries, finely chopped

1 teaspoon minced fresh chives, plus additional for garnish

1 Bring medium saucepan of water to a boil. Gently add eggs with slotted spoon. Reduce heat to maintain a simmer; cook 12 minutes. Meanwhile, prepare ice bath. Drain eggs and place in ice bath; cool 10 minutes.

2 Scoop egg yolks into bowl; reserve whites. Mash yolks with mayonnaise until blended. Stir in curry powder, pepper, salt and paprika; mix well. Stir in cherries and 1 teaspoon chives. Pipe or spoon yolk mixture into egg whites. Garnish with additional chives.

HACKED!

If curry isn't to your taste, you can make a few substitutions for a more classic deviled egg. Omit the curry powder and dried cherries, and save the paprika and chives for a garnish. In step 2, mash the egg yolks with mayonnaise, 1 teaspoon yellow or Dijon mustard, 1 teaspoon white vinegar (or brine from a pickle jar) pepper and salt. Pipe into egg whites; garnish with paprika and chives.

CHOCOLATE CHIP-BANANA MUFFIN BARS

MAKES 8 SERVINGS

   1 package (6½ ounces) chocolate chip muffin mix
   ½ cup water
   1 medium banana, sliced
   ½ cup mini marshmallows
   ½ cup coarsely chopped pecans

1 Preheat oven to 375°F. Spray nonstick 8-inch square baking pan with nonstick cooking spray.

2 Combine muffin mix and water in medium bowl just until blended. Spoon into prepared pan. Layer banana slices over batter; sprinkle with marshmallows and pecans.

3 Bake 30 minutes or until marshmallows begin to brown. Cool completely on wire rack. Cut into 4 squares; cut each square in half diagonally.

HACKED!

This is a good recipe to use a firmer just-ripe banana instead of the softer, overripe ones that work best in banana bread. Bananas with green tips and ridges will ripen at home within a day or two.

SPICED BANANA BREAD

MAKES 1 LOAF

- 1¼ cups all-purpose flour
- ½ cup whole wheat flour
- ½ cup sugar
- 2 teaspoons baking powder
- 2 teaspoons ground cinnamon
- 1 teaspoon ground allspice
- ½ teaspoon ground ginger
- ¼ teaspoon salt
- 2 overripe bananas, mashed
- ½ cup canola oil
- ⅓ cup milk
- ¼ cup unsweetened applesauce
- 1 egg

1 Preheat oven to 350°F. Grease and flour 9×5-inch loaf pan.

2 Combine all-purpose flour, whole wheat flour, sugar, baking powder, cinnamon, allspice, ginger and salt in large bowl.

3 Beat bananas, oil, milk, applesauce and egg in medium bowl with electric mixer at low speed until blended. Gradually add to flour mixture, beating just until moistened. Pour into prepared pan.

4 Bake 45 minutes or until toothpick inserted into center comes out clean. Cool in pan 15 minutes. Remove to wire rack; cool completely.

HACKED!

To speed ripen bananas, place them on a small baking sheet lined with foil. Bake at 300°F for 15 to 20 minutes or until bananas are blackened and very soft. If you don't need ripened bananas immediately but would like them in a few days, place them in a paper bag at room temperature.

BANANA CHOCOLATE-CHUNK CUPCAKES

MAKES 20 CUPCAKES

Ganache Frosting (page 65)
2¼ cups all-purpose flour
2 teaspoons baking powder
1 teaspoon baking soda
½ teaspoon ground cinnamon
¼ teaspoon salt
1 cup sugar
½ cup (1 stick) butter, softened
2 eggs
3 very ripe* bananas, mashed
2 teaspoons vanilla
1 cup sour cream
5 ounces semisweet chocolate, cut into chunks

See page 62 for tips on speed ripening bananas.

1 Prepare frosting. Preheat oven to 350°F. Line 20 standard (2½-inch) muffin cups with paper baking cups. Whisk flour, baking powder, baking soda, cinnamon and salt in medium bowl.

2 Beat sugar and butter in large bowl with electric mixer at medium speed until light and fluffy. Add eggs, one at a time, beating well after each addition. Add bananas and vanilla; beat until blended.

3 Add flour mixture alternately with sour cream, beating until combined. Fold in chocolate chunks. Using ice cream scoop, portion batter into muffin cups.

4 Bake 25 minutes or until toothpick inserted into centers comes out clean. Cool cupcakes in pans on wire racks 10 minutes. Remove to racks; cool completely.

5 Place frosting in pastry bag fitted with medium-size star tip. Pipe rosette on each cupcake.

GANACHE FROSTING
MAKES 1¼ CUPS

- 6 ounces semisweet chocolate, chopped
- 1 tablespoon vanilla
- ¾ cup whipping cream
- 2 tablespoons butter

1 Place chocolate and vanilla in food processor with steel blade. In small saucepan over medium-high heat, bring cream and butter to a simmer, stirring occasionally. Remove from heat.

2 Gradually pour hot cream mixture into processor feed tube and process until smooth and thickened, about 4 minutes. Transfer to small bowl; cover with plastic wrap. Let stand at room temperature 3 hours or until spreadable.

RIPE BANANA MUFFINS

MAKES 1 DOZEN MUFFINS

2 cups whole wheat flour

¾ cup wheat bran (not bran cereal flakes)

¾ cup raw sugar

½ cup wheat germ

2 teaspoons ground cinnamon

1½ teaspoons baking soda

1 teaspoon baking powder

½ teaspoon salt

3 large or 4 medium very ripe* mashed bananas

1 cup plain yogurt

1 egg

3 tablespoons vegetable oil

1 teaspoon vanilla

¾ cup chopped walnuts

¾ cup chocolate chips

⅓ cup raisins

See page 62 for tips on speed ripening bananas.

1 Preheat oven to 350°F. Spray 12 standard (2½-inch) muffin cups with nonstick cooking spray or line with paper baking cups.

2 Whisk flour, wheat bran, sugar, wheat germ, cinnamon, baking soda, baking powder and salt in medium bowl. Combine bananas, yogurt, egg, oil and vanilla in large bowl; stir until well blended. Add dry ingredients; stir just until moistened. Fold in walnuts, chocolate chips and raisins. Using ice cream scoop, potion batter into prepared muffin cups.

3 Bake 18 to 20 minutes or until toothpick inserted into centers comes out clean. Cool in pan on wire rack 5 minutes. Remove from pan; cool on wire rack. Serve warm.

SPICED MAPLE BANANA OATMEAL SMOOTHIE

MAKES 2 SERVINGS

- ½ cup ice
- 1 frozen banana
- ½ cup plain nonfat yogurt
- ¼ cup quick oats
- ¼ cup milk
- 1 tablespoon maple syrup, plus additional for garnish
  Dash of ground cinnamon
  Dash of ground nutmeg
  Whipped cream and cinnamon stick (optional)

1 Combine ice, banana, yogurt, oats, milk, 1 tablespoon maple syrup, cinnamon and nutmeg in blender; blend until smooth.

2 Pour into 2 glasses. Garnish with whipped cream and cinnamon stick. Drizzle with additional maple syrup. Serve immediately.

HACKED!

Frozen bananas have an ice cream-like texture when they're blended, making for the creamiest smoothies. Peel a few bananas and cut them into quarters. Place them on a small baking sheet and freeze overnight or until firm. Transfer them to a freezer food storage bag.

BANANA SPLIT SHAKES

MAKES 4 SERVINGS

- 2 frozen bananas
- ¼ cup milk
- 5 maraschino cherries, drained, plus additional for garnish
- 1 tablespoon chocolate syrup
- ⅛ teaspoon coconut extract
- 4 cups chocolate frozen yogurt

1 Combine bananas, milk, 5 cherries, chocolate syrup and coconut extract in blender. Blend until smooth.

2 Add yogurt, 1 cup at a time; process after each addition until smooth and thick.

3 Pour into 4 glasses. Garnish with additional maraschino cherries. Serve immediately.

BREAKFAST BANANA SPLIT SMOOTHIE

Omit frozen yogurt. Chop 3 large peeled bananas. Spread on baking sheet; freeze until firm. Blend with milk, cherries, chocolate syrup and coconut extract.

PUMPKIN

PUMPKIN AND PARMESAN TWICE-BAKED POTATOES

MAKES 4 SERVINGS

- 2 baking potatoes (12 ounces each)
- 1 cup shredded Parmesan cheese
- 6 tablespoons half-and-half
- ¼ cup canned pumpkin
- 1½ teaspoons minced fresh sage *or* ¼ teaspoon dried thyme
- ¼ teaspoon salt
- ⅛ teaspoon black pepper

1 Preheat oven to 400°F. Scrub potatoes; pierce in several places with fork or small knife. Place potatoes directly on oven rack; bake 1 hour or until soft.

2 When cool enough to handle, cut potatoes in half lengthwise. Scoop out most of potato pulp into medium bowl, leaving thin potato shell. Mash potatoes with fork. Add Parmesan, half-and-half, pumpkin, sage, salt and pepper; mix well.

3 Place potato shells on baking sheet; spoon pumpkin mixture into shells. Bake 10 minutes or until filling is heated through.

HACKED!

Pumpkin may seem like an odd addition to twice baked potatoes, but it makes them extra creamy without using excessive amounts of cheese.

PUMPKIN RAVIOLI

MAKES 2 TO 4 SERVINGS

½ cup canned pumpkin

¼ teaspoon salt

¼ teaspoon black pepper

1 package (14 ounces) wonton wrappers

Whole Italian parsley leaves

2 tablespoons extra virgin olive oil

2 tablespoons butter

2 to 3 cloves garlic, minced

¾ cup shredded Parmesan cheese

2 tablespoons chopped walnuts

1 Combine pumpkin, salt and pepper in medium bowl. Place small bowl of water on work surface.

2 Unwrap wontons; cover with plastic wrap. Place 4 wontons in line on work surface. Brush 2 wontons with water, then place 1 parsley leaf in center of each wonton. Place another wonton over each parsley leaf, pressing out air and sealing edges. Brush 1 layered wonton with water, then place 1 teaspoon pumpkin mixture in center of wonton. Top with remaining layered wonton, pressing out air and sealing edges. Repeat with remaining wontons, parsley leaves and filling.

3 Cut out ravioli using 3-inch round cookie cutter, if desired. Cover with plastic wrap until ready to cook.

4 Bring large pot of salted water to a boil. Working in small batches, slide ravioli into water; cook 1 minute or until ravioli float to surface. Remove from water with slotted spoon; place in medium bowl.

5 Heat oil in large skillet over medium-low heat. Add butter and garlic; cook and stir 1 minute or until garlic is fragrant. Add ravioli; cook over low heat 1 minute or until heated through. Sprinkle with cheese and walnuts; serve immediately.

HACKED!

Wonton wrappers make a perfect substitute for homemade pasta in ravioli recipes. And canned pumpkin makes a super easy filling.

PUMPKIN CURRY

MAKES 4 SERVINGS

1 tablespoon vegetable oil

1 package (14 ounces) extra firm tofu, drained and cut into 1-inch cubes

¼ cup Thai red curry paste

2 cloves garlic, minced

1 can (15 ounces) pumpkin purée

1 can (14 ounces) coconut milk

1 cup water

1½ teaspoons salt

1 teaspoon sriracha sauce

4 cups cut-up vegetables (broccoli, cauliflower, red bell pepper, sweet potato)

½ cup peas

2 cups hot cooked rice

¼ cup shredded fresh basil (optional)

1 Heat oil in wok or large skillet over high heat. Add tofu; stir-fry 2 to 3 minutes or until lightly browned. Add curry paste and garlic; cook and stir 1 minute or until tofu is coated. Add pumpkin, coconut milk, water, salt and sriracha; bring to a boil. Stir in vegetables.

2 Reduce heat to medium; cover and simmer 20 minutes or until vegetables are tender. Stir in peas; cook 1 minute or until heated through. Serve over rice; top with basil, if desired.

HACKED!

If you thought pumpkin was just for pie, think again! It makes a super creamy sauce and pairs well with curry pasta and coconut.

PUMPKIN SPICE LATTE
MAKES 4 SERVINGS

1¾ cups milk, divided

½ cup canned pumpkin

3 tablespoons packed brown sugar

1 teaspoon pumpkin pie spice

1 teaspoon grated fresh ginger

½ teaspoon ground cinnamon, plus additional for garnish

¼ teaspoon salt

⅛ teaspoon coarsely ground black pepper

1 cup strong-brewed hot coffee*

1 tablespoon vanilla

Whipped cream (optional)

Use about 1 tablespoon ground espresso roast or other dark roast coffee for each 3 ounces of water.

1 Combine ½ cup milk, pumpkin, brown sugar, pumpkin pie spice, ginger, ½ teaspoon cinnamon, salt and pepper in medium saucepan; whisk until well blended. Cook over medium-low heat 10 minutes, whisking frequently. Remove from heat; whisk in coffee and vanilla. Strain through fine-mesh strainer into medium bowl.

2 Bring remaining 1¼ cups milk to a simmer in small saucepan over medium-high heat. For froth, whisk vigorously 30 seconds. Whisk into espresso mixture until blended. Garnish with whipped cream and additional cinnamon.

HACKED!

When you're craving a fancy cold-weather coffee drink, save your money and skip the expensive coffee shop. A few pantry staples are all you need to make a delicious copycat recipe at home.

PUMPKIN MAC AND CHEESE

MAKES 6 TO 8 SERVINGS

- 1 package (16 ounces) uncooked large elbow macaroni
- ½ cup (1 stick) butter, divided
- ¼ cup all-purpose flour
- 1½ cups milk
- 1 teaspoon salt, divided
- ¼ teaspoon ground nutmeg
- ⅛ teaspoon ground red pepper
- 2 cups (8 ounces) shredded Cheddar cheese
- 1 cup (4 ounces) shredded Monterey Jack cheese
- 1 cup canned pumpkin
- 1 cup panko bread crumbs
- ½ cup chopped hazelnuts or walnuts (optional)
- ⅛ teaspoon dried sage
- 1 cup (4 ounces) shredded Chihuahua cheese*

If Chihuahua cheese is not available, substitute mozzarella cheese.

1 Preheat oven to 350°F. Spray 2-quart baking dish with nonstick cooking spray. Cook macaroni according to package directions until al dente. Drain and return to saucepan.

2 Melt ¼ cup butter in medium saucepan over medium-high heat. Whisk in flour until smooth; cook 1 minute, whisking constantly. Gradually whisk in milk in thin steady stream. Add ¾ teaspoon salt, nutmeg and ground red pepper; cook 2 to 3 minutes or until thickened, stirring frequently. Gradually add Cheddar and Monterey Jack cheeses, stirring after each addition until smooth. Add pumpkin; cook 1 minute or until heated through, stirring constantly. Pour sauce over pasta; stir to coat.

3 Melt remaining ¼ cup butter in small skillet over medium-low heat; cook until golden brown. Remove from heat; stir in panko, hazelnuts, if desired, sage and remaining ¼ teaspoon salt.

4 Layer half of pasta in prepared baking dish; sprinkle with ½ cup Chihuahua cheese. Top with remaining pasta; sprinkle with remaining Chihuahua cheese. Top with panko mixture.

5 Bake 25 to 30 minutes or until topping is golden brown and pasta is heated through.

CHEESY MASHED POTATO WAFFLES

MAKES 3 SERVINGS

2 cups pre-made or leftover mashed potatoes

1 cup (4 ounces) shredded Cheddar cheese

¼ cup chopped green onions

⅓ cup buttermilk

2 eggs

2 tablespoons butter, melted

½ cup all-purpose flour

1 teaspoon baking powder

½ teaspoon salt

Optional toppings: sour cream, additional shredded Cheddar cheese, additional chopped green onions and/or crumbled cooked bacon

1 Preheat waffle maker to medium.

2 Combine potatoes, cheese, green onions, buttermilk, eggs, butter, flour, baking powder and salt in large bowl; stir well.

3 Scoop 1 cup potato mixture onto waffle maker; spread to cover. Cook about 5 minutes or until golden brown and crisp. Serve with desired toppings.

HACKED!

This section shows you new and fun things to do with your waffle maker that go way beyond plain old waffles.

WAFFLED BURGER SLIDERS

MAKES 8 SLIDERS

  8 ounces lean ground beef
  ½ teaspoon salt
    Black pepper
  8 slider buns *or* 4 slices of bread, cut into quarters and lightly toasted
  1 tablespoon butter, melted
    Toppings: lettuce, tomatoes, cheese, pickles and/or ketchup

1 Combine beef and salt in large bowl. Season with pepper. Shape into 8 small patties.

2 Heat waffle maker to medium. Brush buns with melted butter; set aside.

3 Place four patties in waffle maker. Cook about 3 minutes or until cooked through. Repeat with remaining patties. Serve patties in buns with desired toppings.

QUICK WAFFLED QUESADILLAS

MAKES 2 SERVINGS

 4 (6-inch) flour tortillas

 ¾ cup (3 ounces) shredded Cheddar cheese or Monterey Jack cheese

 ½ cup finely chopped poblano pepper *or* 1 jalapeño pepper, minced

 2 small plum tomatoes, chopped

 ¼ teaspoon ground cumin

 Salt and black pepper

 1 ripe medium avocado, chopped

 4 tablespoons chopped fresh cilantro

 Juice of 1 lime

1 Preheat waffle maker to medium. Coat both sides of each tortilla with nonstick cooking spray.

2 Top 2 tortillas evenly with cheese, poblano pepper, tomato and cumin. Season with salt and pepper. Top with remaining tortillas. Place one quesadilla on waffle maker; close, pressing down slightly. Cook 3 minutes or until golden brown and cheese is melted. Repeat with remaining quesadilla.

3 Cut quesadillas into quarters. Top with avocado, cilantro and lime juice.

TIP

If cheese runs over, let it cool completely in the waffle maker and it will be easy to remove.

WAFFLED PANKO MAC AND CHEESE

MAKES 2 SERVINGS

- 4 ounces uncooked elbow macaroni (about 1 cup)
- 4 slices American cheese
- 1 tablespoon butter
- 1 teaspoon Dijon mustard
  Salt and black pepper
- 1 egg white
- ½ cup plain panko bread crumbs
- 4 teaspoons extra virgin olive oil

- 1 tablespoon chopped fresh parsley

1 Cook macaroni in large saucepan of boiling water according to package directions for al dente. Drain and return to saucepan.

2 Cook and stir cheese, butter and mustard in medium saucepan over low heat until cheese is melted. Season with salt and pepper. Add pasta; mix well.

3 Spread macaroni and cheese in shallow baking pan; cool slightly. Refrigerate about 30 minutes to cool completely.

4 Preheat waffle maker to medium-high heat; spray with nonstick cooking spray.

5 Add egg white and panko to cooled macaroni mixture. Spoon half of the mixture onto waffle maker; close, press down lightly. Cook 4 minutes or until browned and slightly crisp. Gently remove using fork and spatula.

6 Repeat with remaining macaroni mixture. Sprinkle lightly with salt and pepper, if desired. Drizzle with oil and sprinkle with parsley before serving.

BLUEBERRY-ORANGE FRENCH TOAST CASSEROLE

MAKES 6 SERVINGS

- ½ cup sugar
- ½ cup milk
- 2 eggs
- 4 egg whites
- 1 tablespoon grated orange peel
- ½ teaspoon vanilla
- Pinch of salt
- 6 slices whole wheat bread, cut into 1-inch cubes
- 1 cup fresh blueberries
- Maple syrup

1 Coat inside of slow cooker with nonstick cooking spray. Stir sugar and milk in large bowl until sugar is dissolved. Whisk in eggs, egg whites, orange peel, vanilla and salt. Add bread and blueberries; stir to coat.

2 Transfer mixture to slow cooker. Cover; cook on LOW 3 to 4 hours or on HIGH 1½ to 2 hours or until toothpick inserted into center comes out mostly clean.

3 Turn off heat. Let stand 10 minutes. Serve with syrup.

HACKED!

This holiday and brunch favorite can be made in your slow cooker, freeing the oven for other things. And it will leave you plenty of time to prepare other dishes, or to just relax and enjoy some coffee.

STEAMED PORK BUNS

MAKES 16 SERVINGS

½ **(18-ounce) container refrigerated cooked shredded pork in barbecue sauce***

1 **tablespoon Asian garlic chili sauce**

1 **package (about 16 ounces) refrigerated big biscuit dough (8 biscuits)**

Dipping Sauce (recipe follows)

Sliced green onions (optional)

*Look for pork in plain, not smoky, barbecue sauce. Substitute chicken in barbecue sauce, if desired.

1 Combine pork and chili sauce in medium bowl. Split biscuits in half. Roll or stretch each biscuit half into 4-inch circle. Spoon 1 tablespoon pork onto center of each biscuit. Gather edges around filling and press to seal.

2 Generously butter 2-quart baking dish that fits inside of 5- to 6-quart slow cooker. Arrange filled biscuits in single layer, overlapping slightly if necessary. Cover dish with buttered foil, butter side down.

3 Place small rack in slow cooker. Add 1 inch of hot water (water should not touch top of rack). Place baking dish on rack. Cover; cook on HIGH 2 hours.

4 Meanwhile, prepare Dipping Sauce. Garnish pork buns with green onions and serve with Dipping Sauce.

DIPPING SAUCE

Stir together 2 tablespoons rice vinegar, 2 tablespoons soy sauce, 4 teaspoons sugar and 1 teaspoon toasted sesame oil in a small bowl until sugar dissolves. Sprinkle with 1 tablespoon minced green onion just before serving.

HACKED!

Everything about this recipe is a shortcut! Your slow cooker stands in for a steamer, and the bread and filling are both readily available convenience foods used in new ways.

ITALIAN CHEESECAKE

MAKES 16 SERVINGS

9 graham crackers, crushed to fine crumbs

3 tablespoons packed brown sugar

¼ cup (½ stick) butter, melted

2 packages (8 ounces each) cream cheese, softened

1½ cups granulated sugar

1 container (16 ounces) sour cream

1 container (15 ounces) ricotta cheese

1 teaspoon vanilla

4 eggs

3 tablespoons all-purpose flour

3 tablespoons cornstarch

1 Line insert of 5-quart slow cooker with heavy-duty foil. Spray foil with nonstick cooking spray.

2 Combine crushed graham crackers and brown sugar in medium bowl. Stir in melted butter until crumbs hold shape when pinched. Pat firmly into slow cooker. Refrigerate until needed.

3 Beat cream cheese and granulated sugar in large bowl with electric mixer at medium speed until smooth. Add sour cream, ricotta and vanilla; beat until blended. Add eggs, one at a time, beating well after each addition. Beat in flour and cornstarch. Pour filling into prepared crust. Cover; cook on LOW 3 to 4 hours or until cheesecake is nearly set.

4 Turn off heat. Remove lid; cover top of insert with clean kitchen towel. Replace lid; cool 1 hour. Remove insert from base; cool completely. Remove cheesecake using foil. Cover and refrigerate 1 hour or until ready to serve.

HACKED!

The gentle, moist heat of your slow cooker makes a soft, creamy cheesecake with a perfectly smooth top.

FOCACCIA WITH ROSEMARY AND ROMANO

MAKES 1 LOAF

1¼ cups warm water (100° to 110°F)
1 packet (¼ ounce) active dry yeast
3 tablespoons extra virgin olive oil
1 tablespoon sugar
3 to 3½ cups all-purpose flour
1½ tablespoons finely chopped fresh rosemary
1½ teaspoons salt
½ teaspoon red pepper flakes
¼ cup grated Romano cheese

1 Coat inside of slow cooker with nonstick cooking spray. Combine water, yeast, oil and sugar in small bowl; let stand 5 minutes until frothy. Combine flour, rosemary, salt and red pepper flakes in large bowl; stir to blend. Pour water mixture into flour mixture; stir until soft dough forms.

2 Turn dough out onto lightly floured surface; knead 5 minutes. Place dough in slow cooker; stretch to fit bottom. Cover; let stand 1 to 1½ hours in warm place (85°F) until doubled in bulk.

3 Gently press dough with fingertips to deflate. Sprinkle with cheese. Cover; let rise 30 minutes. Place clean kitchen towel over top of insert; replace the lid. Cover; cook on HIGH 2 hours or until dough is lightly browned on sides. Remove to wire rack. Let stand 10 to 15 minutes before slicing.

HACKED!

The slow cooker creates the perfect environment for raising the dough, and the bread bakes up with a surprisingly crispy crust.

NO-FUSS MACARONI AND CHEESE

MAKES 6 TO 8 SERVINGS

2 cups (about 8 ounces) uncooked elbow macaroni

4 ounces pasteurized process cheese product, cubed

1 cup (4 ounces) shredded Cheddar cheese

½ teaspoon salt

⅛ teaspoon black pepper

1½ cups milk

Combine macaroni, cheeses, salt and pepper in slow cooker. Pour milk over top. Cover; cook on LOW 2 to 3 hours, stirring after 20 to 30 minutes.

HACKED!

This is a simple way to make macaroni and cheese without taking the time to boil water and cook noodles. As with all macaroni and cheese dishes, the cheese sauce thickens and begins to dry out as it sits. If it becomes too dry, stir in a little extra milk. Do not cook longer than 4 hours.

PEPPERONI PIZZA MONKEY BREAD

MAKES 12 SERVINGS

- 1 package (about 3 ounces) pepperoni, divided
- 1 teaspoon minced garlic
- ¼ teaspoon red pepper flakes
- 1 package (about 16 ounces) refrigerated biscuits, each biscuit cut into 6 pieces
- 1 can (15 ounces) pizza sauce
- 1 small green bell pepper, chopped
- 1 small yellow bell pepper, chopped
- 1 package (8 ounces) shredded mozzarella cheese

1 Coat inside of round slow cooker with nonstick cooking spray. Prepare foil handles by tearing off four 18×2-inch strips heavy foil (or use regular foil folded to double thickness). Crisscross foil strips in spoke design; place in slow cooker. Spray foil handles with nonstick cooking spray.

2 Chop half of pepperoni slices. Combine chopped pepperoni, garlic and red pepper flakes in medium bowl. Roll each biscuit piece in pepperoni mixture; place in slow cooker. Pour half of pizza sauce over dough. Reserve remaining pizza sauce. Top sauce with bell peppers, mozzarella cheese and remaining half of pepperoni slices.

3 Cover; cook on LOW 3 hours. Turn off heat. Let stand 10 to 15 minutes. Remove from slow cooker using foil handles. Warm remaining pizza sauce; serve with bread for dipping.

MAC AND CHEESE MINI CUPS

MAKES 36 PIECES

- 3 tablespoons butter, divided
- 2 tablespoons all-purpose flour
- 1 cup milk
- 1 teaspoon salt
- ½ teaspoon black pepper
- 1 cup (4 ounces) shredded sharp Cheddar cheese
- 1 cup (4 ounces) shredded Muenster cheese
- 8 ounces elbow macaroni, cooked and drained
- ⅓ cup panko or plain dry bread crumbs

1 Preheat oven to 400°F. Melt 1 tablespoon butter in large saucepan over medium heat; grease 36 mini (1¾-inch) muffin cups with melted butter.

2 Melt remaining 2 tablespoons butter in same saucepan over medium heat. Whisk in flour; cook and stir 2 minutes. Whisk in milk in thin steady stream; cook and stir 3 minutes or until thickened. Remove from heat; stir in cheeses. Stir in macaroni. Divide mixture among prepared muffin cups; sprinkle with panko.

3 Bake about 25 minutes or until golden brown. Cool in pans 10 minutes; remove carefully using sharp knife.

HACKED!

Time to get more out of your muffin pan than just muffins and cupcakes. This chapter will show you the delicious possibilities your muffin pan has to offer.

PUMPKIN TARTLETS

MAKES 12 SERVINGS

- 1 refrigerated pie crust (half of 15-ounce package)
- 1 can (15 ounces) pumpkin purée
- ¼ cup milk
- 1 egg
- 3 tablespoons packed brown sugar
- 3 tablespoons granulated sugar
- ¾ teaspoon ground cinnamon, plus additional for topping
- ½ teaspoon vanilla
- ⅛ teaspoon salt
- ⅛ teaspoon ground nutmeg, plus additional for topping
- Dash ground allspice
- 1½ cups whipped cream or whipped topping

1 Preheat oven to 425°F. Spray 12 standard (2½-inch) muffin cups with nonstick cooking spray.

2 Unroll pie crust on clean work surface. Cut out 12 circles with 2½-inch biscuit cutter; discard scraps. Press one circle into each prepared muffin cup.

3 Whisk pumpkin, milk, egg, brown sugar, granulated sugar, ¾ teaspoon cinnamon, vanilla, salt, ⅛ teaspoon nutmeg and allspice in medium bowl until well blended. Spoon about 2 tablespoons pumpkin mixture into each tartlet shell.

4 Bake 10 minutes. *Reduce oven temperature to 325°F.* Bake 12 to 15 minutes more or until knife inserted into centers comes out clean. Gently remove tarts with small spatula or thin knife; cool completely on wire rack. Spoon 2 tablespoons whipped topping on each tart just before serving. Sprinkle with additional cinnamon and/or nutmeg, if desired.

MINI FRUIT COFFEECAKES
MAKES 12 SERVINGS

1 package (about 17 ounces) frozen puff pastry (2 sheets), thawed

1 package (8 ounces) cream cheese, softened

1 egg

2 tablespoons granulated sugar

12 teaspoons desired fruit filling (apricot jam, strawberry jam, lemon curd or a combination)

½ cup powdered sugar

2 teaspoons milk

1 Preheat oven to 350°F. Spray 12 standard (2½-inch) muffin cups with nonstick cooking spray.

2 Unroll puff pastry on work surface; cut each sheet into 6 rectangles. Fit pastry into prepared muffin cups, pressing into bottoms and up sides. (Two sides of each rectangle will extend up over top of muffin pan.)

3 Beat cream cheese in large bowl with electric mixer at medium-high speed until smooth. Add egg and granulated sugar; beat until well blended. Spoon heaping tablespoon cream cheese mixture into each cup; top with 1 teaspoon filling. Snip center of each overhanging pastry with scissors or paring knife; fold resulting 4 flaps in over filling, overlapping slightly (as you would fold a box).

4 Bake 20 minutes or until pastry is golden and filling is set and puffed. Cool in pan 2 minutes; remove to wire rack.

5 Meanwhile, whisk powdered sugar and milk in small bowl until smooth. Drizzle glaze over coffeecakes.

QUICK AND EASY ARANCINI

MAKES 12 ARANCINI

> 1 package (6 to 8 ounces) sun-dried tomato, mushroom or Milanese risotto mix, plus ingredients to prepare mix*
>
> ½ cup frozen peas *or* ¼ cup finely chopped oil-packed sun-dried tomatoes (optional)
>
> ½ cup panko bread crumbs
>
> ¼ cup finely shredded or grated Parmesan cheese
>
> 2 tablespoons minced fresh parsley
>
> 2 tablespoons butter, melted
>
> 4 ounces Swiss, Asiago or fontina cheese, cut into 12 cubes (about ½ inch)
>
> **Or use 3 cups leftover risotto.*

1 Prepare risotto according to package directions. Stir in peas, if desired. Let stand, uncovered, 20 minutes or until thickened and cool enough to handle.

2 Preheat oven to 375°F. Spray 12 standard (2½-inch) muffin pan cups with nonstick cooking spray. Combine panko, Parmesan, parsley and melted butter in medium bowl.

3 Shape level ¼ cupfuls risotto into balls around Swiss cheese cubes, covering completely. Roll in panko mixture to coat. Place in prepared muffin cups.

4 Bake 15 minutes or until arancini are golden brown and cheese cubes are melted. Cool in pan 5 minutes. Serve warm.

HACKED!

Arancini, a southern Italian specialty, are typically fried. This version simplifies the cooking method by using a muffin pan, and the risotto by using a packaged mix. For an easy variation, substitute ½ cup chopped ham for the peas.

CHOCOLATE CHIP COOKIE DELIGHTS
MAKES 18 SERVINGS

- 1¾ cups all-purpose flour
- ¾ teaspoon salt
- ¾ teaspoon baking powder
- ½ teaspoon baking soda
- 10 tablespoons (1¼ sticks) butter, softened
- ½ cup plus 2 tablespoons packed brown sugar
- ½ cup granulated sugar
- 1 egg
- 1 teaspoon vanilla
- 1½ cups semisweet or bittersweet chocolate chips
- Coarse or flaked salt (optional)
- Vanilla ice cream (optional)

1 Preheat oven to 375°F. Spray 18 standard (2½-inch) muffin cups with nonstick cooking spray.

2 Combine flour, ¾ teaspoon salt, baking powder and baking soda in small bowl; mix well. Combine butter, brown sugar and granulated sugar in large bowl; beat with electric mixer at medium-high speed about 5 minutes or until very light and fluffy. Add egg; beat until blended. Beat in vanilla. Stir in flour mixture until blended. Stir in chocolate chips. Spoon scant ¼ cup dough into each prepared muffin cup; sprinkle with coarse salt, if desired.

3 Bake about 14 minutes or until edges are golden brown but centers are still soft. Cool in pans 5 minutes; invert onto wire rack. Turn cookies right side up; serve warm with ice cream, if desired.

HACKED!

What's better than a warm chocolate chip cookie? A perfectly round, deep cookie with an extra chocolatey, gooey center—it's like a miniature skillet cookie.

TORTILLA CUPS WITH CORN AND BLACK BEAN SALAD

MAKES 6 SERVINGS

3 tablespoons vegetable oil, divided

1 teaspoon salt, divided

½ teaspoon chili powder

6 (6-inch) flour tortillas

1 cup corn

1 cup chopped red bell pepper

1 cup canned black beans, rinsed and drained

1 small ripe avocado, diced

¼ cup lime juice

¼ cup chopped fresh cilantro

1 small jalapeño pepper, seeded and minced

1 Preheat oven to 350°F. Spray 6 standard (2½-inch) muffin cups with nonstick cooking spray. Whisk 1 tablespoon oil, ½ teaspoon salt and chili powder in small bowl until well blended.

2 Stack tortillas; wrap loosely in waxed paper. Microwave on HIGH 10 to 15 seconds or just until softened. Brush one side of each tortilla lightly with oil mixture; press into prepared cups, oiled side up.

3 Bake about 10 minutes or until edges are golden brown. Cool in pan 2 minutes; remove to wire rack. Cool completely.

4 Combine corn, bell pepper, beans and avocado in large bowl. Whisk remaining 2 tablespoons oil, ½ teaspoon salt, lime juice, cilantro and jalapeño in small bowl until well blended. Add to corn mixture; toss gently to coat. Fill tortilla cups with salad. Serve immediately. (Tortilla cups and salad can be prepared ahead of time; fill cups just before serving.)

HACKED!

For slightly larger tortilla cups, use the back of the muffin pan instead. Spray the back of a 12-cup muffin pan with nonstick cooking spray. Soften the tortillas and brush with the oil mixture, then fit them between the cups on the back of the muffin pan. (Only about 3 will fit at one time, so 2 batches is required.) Bake at 350°F about 8 minutes or until edges are golden brown.

CORN FRITTERS

MAKES 8 TO 9 FRITTERS

- 2 large ears corn
- 2 eggs, separated
- ¼ cup all-purpose flour
- 1 tablespoon sugar
- 1 tablespoon butter, melted
- ¼ teaspoon salt
- ⅛ teaspoon black pepper
- ⅛ teaspoon cream of tartar
- 1 to 2 tablespoons vegetable oil

1 Husk corn. Cut kernels from ears (1½ to 2 cups); place in medium bowl. Hold cobs over bowl, scraping with back of knife to extract juice. Transfer about half of kernels to food processor; process 2 to 3 seconds or until coarsely chopped. Add to whole kernels.

2 Whisk egg yolks in large bowl. Whisk in flour, sugar, butter, salt and pepper. Stir in corn mixture.

3 Beat egg whites and cream of tartar in separate large bowl with electric mixer at high speed until stiff peaks form. Fold egg whites into corn mixture.

4 Heat 1 tablespoon oil in 12-inch nonstick skillet over medium-high heat. Drop ¼ cupfuls of batter into skillet 1 inch apart. Cook 3 to 5 minutes per side or until lightly browned. Repeat with remaining batter, adding more oil, if necessary. Serve hot.

HACKED!

The easiest (and neatest) way to remove kernels from a cob? With a bundt pan! Place the stem end of a husked ear of corn, securely in the hold of the bundt pan. Scrape the kernels off with a knife, letting them fall into the pan. The pan keeps the ear secure and collects the kernels and any juice.

CHILI CORN BREAD
MAKES 12 SERVINGS

- ¼ cup chopped red bell pepper
- ¼ cup chopped green bell pepper
- 2 small jalapeño peppers, minced
- 2 cloves garlic, minced
- ¾ cup corn from 2 ears of corn (see note on page 115)
- 1½ cups yellow cornmeal
- ½ cup all-purpose flour
- 2 tablespoons sugar
- 2 teaspoons baking powder
- ½ teaspoon baking soda
- ½ teaspoon ground cumin
- ½ teaspoon salt
- 1½ cups buttermilk
- 1 egg
- 2 egg whites
- ¼ cup (½ stick) butter, melted

1 Preheat oven to 375°F. Spray 8-inch square baking pan with nonstick cooking spray.

2 Spray small skillet with cooking spray. Add bell peppers, jalapeños and garlic; cook and stir over medium heat 3 to 4 minutes or until peppers are tender. Stir in corn; cook 1 to 2 minutes. Remove from heat.

3 Combine cornmeal, flour, sugar, baking powder, baking soda, cumin and salt in large bowl. Add buttermilk, egg, egg whites and butter; mix until blended. Stir in corn mixture. Pour batter into prepared baking pan.

4 Bake 25 to 30 minutes or until golden brown. Cool on wire rack. Cut into 12 squares before serving.

CORN CHOWDER

MAKES 6 SERVINGS

1 tablespoon butter

1 red bell pepper, diced

1 medium onion, diced

1 stalk celery, sliced

2 cans (about 14 ounces each) vegetable broth

2 cups corn from 6 to 8 ears (see note on page 115)

3 small potatoes, peeled and cut into ½-inch pieces

½ teaspoon salt

½ teaspoon black pepper

¼ teaspoon ground coriander

½ cup whipping cream

8 slices bacon, crisp-cooked and crumbled

1 Melt butter in large saucepan over medium-high heat. Add bell pepper, onion and celery; cook 5 to 7 minutes or until vegetables are softened, stirring occasionally.

2 Add broth, corn, potatoes, salt, black pepper and coriander; bring to a boil. Reduce heat to low; cover and simmer 30 minutes or until vegetables are very tender.

3 Partially mash soup mixture with potato masher to thicken. Stir in cream; cook over medium heat until hot. Adjust seasonings. Garnish with bacon.

HACKED!

Speaking of corn, did you know that you can cook a whole cob in just minutes, no boiling water required? Simply husk the corn and remove the silk, then wrap it in a paper towel. Put it in the microwave and cook it on HIGH for 2 to 3 minutes or until tender.

EASY CHEESY BACON BREAD

MAKES 12 SERVINGS

- 1 pound bacon, chopped
- 1 onion, chopped
- 1 green bell pepper, chopped
- ½ teaspoon ground red pepper
- 3 packages (7½ ounces each) refrigerated buttermilk biscuits, separated and quartered
- 2½ cups (10 ounces) shredded Cheddar cheese, divided
- ½ cup (1 stick) butter, melted

1 Preheat oven to 350°F. Spray nonstick bundt pan with nonstick cooking spray.

2 Cook bacon in large skillet over medium heat until crisp. Drain on paper towels. Reserve 1 tablespoon drippings in skillet. Add onion, bell pepper and ground red pepper; cook and stir over medium-high heat 10 minutes or until tender. Cool.

3 Combine biscuit pieces, bacon, onion mixture, 2 cups cheese and melted butter in large bowl; mix gently. Place mixture in prepared bundt pan.

4 Bake 30 minutes or until golden brown. Cool in pan 5 minutes. Invert onto serving platter and sprinkle with remaining ½ cup cheese. Serve warm.

HUEVOS RAMENCHEROS
MAKES 8 SERVINGS

2 packages (3 ounces each) chicken-flavored ramen noodles, broken into small pieces

8 eggs

1½ cups milk

1 teaspoon ground cumin

1½ cups (6 ounces) shredded sharp Cheddar cheese, divided

1 cup finely chopped green onions, divided

1 poblano pepper, seeded and diced

1 can (about 15 ounces) black beans, rinsed and drained

¼ cup chopped white onions

¼ cup chopped green bell pepper

¼ cup chopped tomato

2 limes, quartered

1 cup salsa

1 Preheat oven to 350°F. Spray nonstick bundt pan with nonstick cooking spray.

2 Cook ramen noodles according to package directions. Drain and rinse under cold water to stop cooking.

3 Whisk eggs, milk, seasoning packets and cumin in medium bowl until well blended. Whisk in 1 cup cheese and ½ cup green onions. Sprinkle poblano pepper in bottom of prepared pan, top with noodles, then pour egg mixture evenly over all. Bake 45 minutes or until knife inserted into center comes out clean. Cool on wire rack 15 minutes.

4 Meanwhile, place beans in medium microwavable bowl. Add white onions, bell pepper and tomato. Cover and microwave on HIGH 2 minutes or until heated through.

5 Place plate on top of pan; carefully flip to remove. Sprinkle top with remaining cheese and green onions. Spoon bean mixture in center hole; garnish with lime wedges and serve with salsa.

BUTTERMILK DROP BISCUITS

MAKES 9 BISCUITS

- 2 cups all-purpose flour
- 2 teaspoons baking powder
- 1 teaspoon sugar
- ½ teaspoon salt
- ¼ teaspoon baking soda
- 1 cup buttermilk
- 5 tablespoons butter, melted, divided

1 Preheat oven to 450°F. Spray baking sheet with nonstick cooking spray.

2 Combine flour, baking powder, sugar, salt and baking soda in large bowl; mix well. Whisk buttermilk and 4 tablespoons butter in small bowl until well blended. Stir into flour mixture just until combined.

3 Spray ¼-cup ice cream scoop or 3-tablespoon cookie scoop with nonstick cooking spray. Scoop batter into mounds with ice cream scoop and drop 1½ inches apart onto prepared baking sheet.

4 Bake 12 minutes or until tops are golden brown. Brush tops with remaining 1 tablespoon butter. Cool on baking sheets 5 minutes; serve warm or cool completely.

HACKED!

Use an ice cream scoop with a release lever to perfectly portion biscuit dough and cupcake batter. You can even use it to make perfectly round scoops when serving mashed potatoes, rice, pasta salad and potato salad. You can also use a large cookie scoop but depending on what you're scooping, you'll probably want to use a heaping scoopful to make up for the smaller volume.

CREAM CHEESE CUPCAKES

MAKES 24 CUPCAKES

- 3 packages (8 ounces each) cream cheese, softened
- 5 eggs
- 1¼ cups sugar, divided
- 2½ teaspoons vanilla, divided
- 1 container (16 ounces) sour cream
- 1 cup chopped fresh pitted cherries, fresh blueberries and/or canned crushed pineapple, drained

1 Preheat oven to 325°F. Line 24 standard (2½-inch) muffin cups with paper baking cups.

2 Beat cream cheese, eggs, 1 cup sugar and 1½ teaspoons vanilla in large bowl with electric mixer at medium speed 2 minutes or until well blended. Using ice cream scoop, evenly portion batter into muffin cups.

3 Bake 20 minutes or until light golden brown. Cool cupcakes in pans 5 minutes. (Centers of cupcakes will sink slightly.) Do not remove cupcakes from pans.

4 Meanwhile, combine sour cream, remaining ¼ cup sugar and 1 teaspoon vanilla in medium bowl; stir until blended. Top cupcakes evenly with sour cream mixture. Bake 5 minutes. Cool in pans 10 minutes. Remove to wire racks; cool completely. Top with fruit.

HACKED!

An ice cream scoop with a release lever is a great tool for perfectly filled muffin cups. Scoop a heaping mound of batter into each prepared muffin cup. If there's any remaining batter left, fill additional muffin cups or add a bit more batter to each cup with a small spoon.

SWEET AND SAVORY BREAKFAST MUFFINS

MAKES 12 MUFFINS

1¼ cups original pancake and baking mix

1 cup milk

3 egg whites

¼ cup maple syrup

4 small fully cooked turkey breakfast sausage links, diced

1 cup fresh blueberries

1 Preheat oven to 375°F. Spray 12 standard (2½-inch) muffin cups with nonstick cooking spray.

2 Stir pancake mix, milk, egg whites and maple syrup in large bowl until smooth and well blended. Fold in sausage and blueberries. Using ice cream scoop, portion batter into muffin cups.

3 Bake 18 to 20 minutes or until toothpick inserted into centers comes out clean. Serve warm.

LEFTOVER CANDY CUPCAKES WITH PEANUT BUTTER FROSTING

MAKES 24 CUPCAKES

- 15 to 20 pieces chocolate peanut butter cup candy, divided
- 1 package (about 15 ounces) chocolate cake mix, plus ingredients to prepare mix
- ½ cup (1 stick) butter, softened
- ½ cup creamy peanut butter (not natural)
- 4 to 5 teaspoons vanilla
- 1 to 2 cups powdered sugar

1 Grease or line 24 standard (2½-inch) muffin cups with paper baking cups. Cut 12 pieces of candy in half. Prepare cake mix according to package directions. Using ice cream scoop, portion batter into prepared muffin cups, filling half full. Place 1 piece of chopped candy in center, on top of batter. Spoon remaining batter on top of candy.

2 Bake according to package directions until toothpick inserted into centers comes out clean. Cool in pan 10 minutes. Remove to wire racks; cool completely.

3 Meanwhile for frosting, beat butter in medium bowl with electric mixer at medium speed until light and fluffy. Add peanut butter and vanilla; beat 2 minutes or until fluffy. Gradually beat in powdered sugar, ¼ cup at a time until frosting is spreadable consistency. Spread frosting over cupcakes; top with remaining chopped candy.

HACKED!

Put leftover candy to good use by transforming it into another dessert. Use any kind of chocolate bar candy, or use a combination to make surprise cupcakes.

CAKE BONBONS

MAKES ABOUT 30 BONBONS

> 4 cups lightly packed fresh cake crumbs
>
> ¼ cup frosting
>
> 1½ to 3 teaspoons liqueur or whipping cream
>
> 2 bars (4 ounces each) 60 to 70% bittersweet chocolate, coarsely chopped
>
> Optional toppings: unsweetened cocoa powder, powdered sugar, finely chopped nuts, colored sprinkles or finely crushed cookie crumbs

1 Combine crumbs, frosting and liqueur in medium bowl. Gently mix together until evenly blended. If mixture seems dry, add more liqueur, 1 teaspoon at a time.

2 Shape mixture into 1-inch balls, rolling between palms until evenly shaped. Place on waxed paper.

3 Carefully melt chocolate in double boiler over low heat; do not let water splash into chocolate. Or melt chocolate in glass measuring cup in microwave on MEDIUM (50%) 60 to 90 seconds. Stir; continue to microwave at 30-second intervals, stirring until chocolate has melted completely. (Reheat on MEDIUM, if necessary.)

4 Place cake ball on skewer and dip completely into chocolate. Tap skewer gently to let excess chocolate drip back into double boiler; place coated ball on waxed paper. Repeat with remaining cake balls. If desired, roll in toppings. Let stand until chocolate cools.

HACKED!

If you have leftover cupcakes or frosted cake, crumble them up with the frosting and mix well. If the cake and frosting don't stick together, add additional frosting or a small amount of milk until the mixture holds together when pressed.

ITALIAN CROUTON SALAD

MAKES 6 SERVINGS

 6 ounces leftover stale French or Italian bread
 ¼ cup plain yogurt
 ¼ cup red wine vinegar
 4 teaspoons olive oil
 1 tablespoon water
 3 cloves garlic, minced
 6 medium plum tomatoes, sliced (about 3¾ to 4 cups)
 ½ medium red onion, thinly sliced
 3 tablespoons sliced fresh basil
 2 tablespoons finely chopped fresh parsley
 12 red lettuce leaves *or* 4 cups prepared Italian salad mix
 2 tablespoons grated Parmesan cheese

1 Preheat broiler. To prepare croutons, cut bread into ¾-inch cubes.
  Place in single layer on baking sheet. Broil 4 inches from heat
  3 minutes or until bread is golden, stirring every 30 seconds to
  1 minute. Place croutons in large bowl.

2 Whisk together yogurt, vinegar, oil, water and garlic in small bowl
  until blended. Add tomatoes, onion, basil and parsley to croutons;
  stir to combine. Pour yogurt mixture over crouton mixture; toss to
  coat. Cover; refrigerate 30 minutes or up to 1 day. (Croutons will be
  softer the following day.)

3 To serve, place lettuce on serving plates. Top with crouton mixture;
  sprinkle with cheese.

TROPICAL TURKEY SALAD

MAKES 6 SERVINGS

4 cups cubed cooked leftover turkey

2 cups diced ripe mango (2 medium mangoes)

1 cup pecan pieces, toasted*

¾ cup mayonnaise

1 tablespoon lime juice

1 teaspoon poppy seeds

½ teaspoon salt

¼ teaspoon black pepper

6 cups greens, such as Bibb lettuce or spinach leaves

To toast pecans, spread in single layer in large heavy skillet. Cook over medium heat 3 to 5 minutes or until nuts are lightly browned and fragrant, stirring frequently. Remove from skillet immediately. Cool before using.

1 Combine turkey, mangoes and pecans in large bowl. Combine mayonnaise, lime juice, poppy seeds, salt and pepper in small bowl until well blended. Pour over turkey mixture; gently stir until coated.

2 Arrange greens on plates. Spoon turkey salad over greens. Serve immediately or cover and refrigerate up to 4 hours.

HACKED!

Give your Thanksgiving leftovers a tropical makeover for a nice change of pace from cranberries and sage. You might even have some leftover pecans around from your sweet potato casserole.

LEFTOVER CANDY ICE CREAM SUNDAE WITH HARD CHOCOLATE TOPPING

MAKES 4 SERVINGS

1 pint vanilla ice cream, slightly softened
½ to 1 cup chopped leftover Halloween candy
1 cup semisweet chocolate chips
2 tablespoons coconut oil

1 For ice cream, mix ice cream and candy in large bowl until combined. Cover bowl with plastic wrap; return to freezer to harden.

2 Meanwhile, prepare chocolate sauce. Combine chocolate chips and oil in medium microwavable bowl. Microwave on HIGH 30 seconds; stir. Microwave at additional 30-second intervals until melted and smooth.

3 Scoop ice cream into bowls. Pour chocolate sauce over ice cream. Allow to sit 30 seconds for sauce to harden.

HACKED!

Another great use for Halloween, Easter and Valentine's Day candy, this sundae is easy to make and easy to customize.

NOT-SO-SLOPPY JOES

MAKES 6 SERVINGS

- 1 **pound ground beef or turkey**
- ⅓ **cup finely chopped onion**
- ⅓ **cup shredded carrot**
- 1 **can (8 ounces) tomato sauce, divided**
- 1 **egg**
- ½ **teaspoon salt**
- ½ **teaspoon dried Italian seasoning**
- ⅛ **teaspoon black pepper**
- 6 **hot dog buns**
- 6 **slices mozzarella cheese, halved**

1 Preheat oven to 350°F. Spray 13×9-inch baking pan with nonstick cooking spray.

2 Combine ground beef, onion, carrot, half of tomato sauce, egg, salt, Italian seasoning and pepper in large bowl. Shape mixture into 1½-inch balls. Place meatballs in prepared pan; top with remaining half of tomato sauce. Bake 15 to 20 minutes or until meatballs are browned and cooked through. Cover with foil to keep warm.

3 Open buns and arrange on baking sheet. Place 2 cheese halves on bottom of each bun. Heat 5 minutes or until cheese melts. Spoon meatballs and sauce into each bun.

HACKED!

Kids love Sloppy Joes, but they're so messy. This recipe solves that problem by turning the mess into meatballs.

SAUSAGE SPAGHETTI
MAKES 4 SERVINGS

> 1 package (about 14 ounces) smoked sausage
> 8 ounces uncooked thick spaghetti or regular spaghetti
> ¼ cup olive oil or butter
> 2 cloves garlic, minced
> ¼ cup Parmesan cheese
> Salt, black pepper and red pepper flakes

1 Cut sausage into ¼-inch slices. Stick 5 spaghetti noodles into each slice.

2 Bring large saucepan of water to a boil. Add pasta; push fully into water as noodles soften. Cook 9 to 10 minutes or until pasta is tender, stirring frequently to prevent sticking.

3 Heat oil in large saucepan over medium heat. Add garlic; cook 30 seconds. Add pasta and sausage; toss to coat. Remove from heat; top with cheese. Season with salt, black pepper and red pepper flakes.

VARIATIONS

For an Italian version, use smoked Italian sausage instead of regular smoked sausage and top with marinara sausage. For a cheesy version, melt 2 tablespoons butter in medium saucepan over medium-high heat. Whisk in 2 tablespoons flour until smooth and well blended; cook 1 minute without browning. Gradually whisk in 1½ cups milk; cook until thickened, stirring frequently. Whisk in 8 ounces shredded cheese (American, Cheddar, Monterey Jack, Swiss or a combination) until melted and smooth. Season with salt. Pour sauce over pasta; stir to coat.

MEAT LOAF CUPCAKES

MAKES 10 SERVINGS

  3 medium potatoes, peeled and chopped

1½ pounds 90% lean ground beef

  ½ cup finely chopped onion

  ⅓ cup old-fashioned oats

  1 egg

  2 tablespoons chopped fresh rosemary

1¼ teaspoons salt, divided

  ¼ teaspoon black pepper

  ½ cup milk

  2 tablespoons butter

  ¼ cup snipped fresh chives

1 Preheat oven to 350°F. Place potatoes in medium saucepan; cover with water. Bring to a boil; cook 25 to 30 minutes or until potatoes are fork-tender.

2 Combine beef, onion, oats, egg, rosemary ½ teaspoon salt and pepper in large bowl; mix well. Divide mixture among 10 standard (2½-inch) muffin cups or silicone liners.

3 Bake 25 minutes or until cooked through (160°F). Meanwhile, beat potatoes, milk, butter and remaining ¾ teaspoon salt in large bowl with electric mixer at medium speed 3 minutes or until smooth. Place mashed potatoes in large piping bag fitted with large star tip. Pipe potatoes over meat loaves. Sprinkle with chives.

HACKED!

Surprise your kids with cupcakes for dinner. Although not the dessert cupcakes they'd probably rather have, these mini meat loaves in disguise are tasty enough that they won't mind.

WILD WATERMELON POPS

MAKES 4 POPS

2 cups diced seedless watermelon (1-inch cubes)
2 tablespoons strawberry fruit spread
1 cup vanilla frozen yogurt
4 (5-ounce) paper or plastic cups or pop molds
4 teaspoons mini semisweet chocolate chips
4 pop sticks

1 Combine 1 cup watermelon and fruit spread in blender or food processor; blend until smooth. Add remaining 1 cup watermelon; blend until smooth and well combined. Add frozen yogurt, ½ cup at a time, blending until smooth after each addition.

2 Pour mixture into cups (see below). Freeze 1 hour or until mixture just begins to harden.

3 Stir mixture in cups until smooth and slushy. Stir 1 teaspoon chocolate chips into each cup. Smooth top of mixture with back of spoon. Cover top of each cup with small piece of foil. Freeze 1 hour.

4 Insert sticks through center of foil. Freeze 4 hours or until firm.

5 To serve, remove foil and peel away paper cups or gently twist frozen pops out of plastic cups.

HACKED!

Turn watermelon into a frozen treat with seeds that you'll actually want to eat. To use cone-shaped paper cups, line a baking sheet with regular-shaped 5-ounce paper cups, bottom sides up. Cut a small hole in the bottom of each regular-shaped paper cup. Place a cone-shaped cup, tip side down, in the hole to hold the pop in place.

ICE CREAM CONE CUPCAKES

MAKES 24 CUPCAKES

24 flat-bottomed ice cream cones

1 package (about 15 ounces) white cake mix, plus ingredients to prepare mix

2 tablespoons rainbow nonpareils

Prepared vanilla and chocolate frostings

Additional nonpareils and decors

1 Preheat oven to 350°F. Stand ice cream cones in 13×9-inch baking pans or muffin cups.

2 Prepare cake mix according to package directions; stir in 2 tablespoons nonpareils. Spoon batter evenly into cones.

3 Bake 20 minutes or until toothpick inserted into centers comes out clean. Remove to wire racks; cool completely.

4 Frost cupcakes and decorate as desired.

HACKED!

These "ice cream cones" are the perfect summer party treat because they'll never melt. To make them double "scoops," skip the frosting and top cakes with ice cream. Decorate with quick-hardening chocolate topping, cherries and desired decors. These cupcakes are best the day they're made.

COOKIE SUNDAE CUPS

MAKES 1½ DOZEN CUPS

1 package (about 16 ounces) refrigerated chocolate chip cookie dough
6 cups (1½ quarts) ice cream, any flavor
Ice cream topping, any flavor
Whipped cream
Colored sprinkles

1 Preheat oven to 350°F. Lightly grease 18 standard (2½-inch) muffin cups.

2 Shape dough into 18 balls; press onto bottoms and up sides of prepared muffin cups.

3 Bake 14 to 18 minutes or until golden brown. Cool in pans on wire racks 10 minutes. Remove to wire racks; cool completely.

4 Place ⅓ cup ice cream in each cookie cup. Drizzle with ice cream topping. Top with whipped cream and sprinkles.

HACKED!

Up your sundae game with these easy cookie cups. To make them for a party, prepare the cups in advance and scoop the ice cream onto a baking sheet and place in the freezer. When you're ready to serve, place the scoops of ice cream on the cookies and garnish as desired. You'll have dessert ready in no time!

BROCCOLI SURPRISE CORN MUFFINS

MAKES 12 MUFFINS

- 1 small broccoli crown, broken into florets
- 2 tablespoons water
- 1 cup all-purpose flour
- 1 cup cornmeal
- ¼ cup sugar
- 2 teaspoons baking powder
- 1 teaspoon salt
- 1 cup milk
- 2 eggs
- ¼ cup (½ stick) butter, melted

1 Preheat oven to 400°F. Grease 12 standard (2½-inch) muffin cups or line with paper baking cups. Place broccoli and water in microwavable dish. Cover; cook on HIGH 2 minutes or until crisp-tender.

2 Whisk flour, cornmeal, sugar, baking powder and salt in medium bowl. Whisk milk, eggs and butter in large bowl. Add flour mixture; stir just until combined. Spoon 1 tablespoon batter into each prepared muffin cup. Place one piece of broccoli in each cup. Top evenly with remaining batter.

3 Bake 15 minutes or until toothpick inserted into centers comes out clean. Cool in pan 5 minutes. Remove to wire rack. Serve warm or at room temperature.

A

Asparagus: Ham and Asparagus Quiche, 48

B

Bacon

Bacon and Egg Cups, 42
Breakfast Flats, 36
Caramelized Bacon, 44
Chocolate-Covered Bacon, 46
Corn Chowder, 118
Easy Cheesy Bacon Bread, 120

Bacon and Egg Cups, 42
Bacon and Egg Wraps, 52
Banana Chocolate-Chunk Cupcakes, 64

Bananas

Banana Chocolate-Chunk Cupcakes, 64
Banana Split Shakes, 70
Breakfast Banana Split Smoothie, 70
Chocolate Chip-Banana Muffin Bars, 60
Ripe Banana Muffins, 66
Spiced Banana Bread, 62
Spiced Maple Banana Oatmeal Smoothie, 68

Banana Split Shakes, 70

Beef and Pork

Meat Loaf Cupcakes, 144
Not-So-Sloppy Joes, 140
Sausage Spaghetti, 142
Steamed Pork Buns, 92
Waffled Burger Sliders, 84

Biscuit Dough

Cookie Dough Monkey Bread, 10
Easy Cheesy Bacon Bread, 120
Mini Biscuit Doughnuts, 6
Pepperoni Pizza Monkey Bread, 100

Biscuit Dough *(continued)*

Quick Jelly-Filled Biscuit Doughnuts, 8
Steamed Pork Buns, 92
Super Simple Cheesy Bubble Loaf, 12

Blueberry-Orange French Toast Casserole, 90

Breakfast

Bacon and Egg Wraps, 52
Blueberry-Orange French Toast Casserole, 90
Breakfast Banana Split Smoothie, 70
Breakfast Flats, 36
Cheddar, Broccoli and Mushroom Quiche, 50
Chocolate Chip-Banana Muffin Bars, 60
Easy Eggs Benedict, 54
Ham and Asparagus Quiche, 48
Mini Biscuit Doughnuts, 6
Mini Fruit Coffeecakes, 106
Quick Jelly-Filled Biscuit Doughnuts, 8
Ramen Egg Cups, 16
Ramen French Toast, 20
Ripe Banana Muffins, 66
Spiced Maple Banana Oatmeal Smoothie, 68
Sweet and Savory Breakfast Muffins, 128

Breakfast Banana Split Smoothie, 70
Breakfast Flats, 36

Broccoli

Broccoli Surprise Corn Muffins, 152
Cheddar, Broccoli and Mushroom Quiche, 50
Tahini Lentil Ramen Salad, 24

Broccoli Surprise Corn Muffins, 152

Bundt Pan
    Cookie Dough Monkey Bread, 10
    Easy Cheesy Bacon Bread, 120
    Huevos Ramencheros, 122
Buttermilk Drop Biscuits, 124

C
Cake Bonbons, 132
Cake Mix
    Ice Cream Cone Cupcakes, 148
    Leftover Candy Cupcakes with Peanut Butter Frosting, 130
    Minty Cookies and Cream Cake, 34
    Mixed Berry Dump Cake, 30
    PB & J Sandwich Cake, 26
    Peach Strawberry Dump Cake, 28
    Rainbow Cake, 32
Cakes
    Cake Bonbons, 132
    Minty Cookies and Cream Cake, 34
    PB & J Sandwich Cake, 26
    Peach Strawberry Dump Cake, 28
    Rainbow Cake, 32
Caramelized Bacon, 44
Cheddar, Broccoli and Mushroom Quiche, 50
Cheese
    Bacon and Egg Cups, 42
    Breakfast Flats, 36
    Cheddar, Broccoli and Mushroom Quiche, 50
    Cheesy Mashed Potato Waffles, 82
    Easy Cheesy Bacon Bread, 120
    Focaccia with Rosemary and Romano, 96
    Ham and Asparagus Quiche, 48
    Huevos Ramencheros, 122

Cheese *(continued)*
    Mac and Cheese Mini Cups, 102
    No-Fuss Macaroni and Cheese, 98
    Pepperoni Pizza Monkey Bread, 100
    Pepperoni Pizza Rolls, 38
    Pepperoni Puffers, 22
    Pumpkin and Parmesan Twice-Baked Potatoes, 72
    Pumpkin Mac and Cheese, 80
    Quick and Easy Arancini, 108
    Quick Waffled Quesadillas, 86
    Ramen Bites on a Stick, 18
    Sausage and Kale Deep-Dish Mini Pizzas, 40
    Super Simple Cheesy Bubble Loaf, 12
    Waffled Panko Mac and Cheese, 88
Cheesy Mashed Potato Waffles, 82
Chili Corn Bread, 116
Chocolate
    Banana Chocolate-Chunk Cupcakes, 64
    Banana Split Shakes, 70
    Cake Bonbons, 132
    Chocolate Chip Cookie Delights, 110
    Chocolate-Covered Bacon, 46
    Cookie Dough Monkey Bread, 10
    Ganache Frosting, 65
    Leftover Candy Cupcakes with Peanut Butter Frosting, 130
    Leftover Candy Ice Cream Sundae with Hard Chocolate Topping, 138

Chocolate *(continued)*
Minty Cookies and Cream Cake,
34
Ripe Banana Muffins, 66
Chocolate Chip Cookie Delights,
110
Chocolate Chip-Banana Muffin
Bars, 60
Chocolate-Covered Bacon, 46
Cinnamon-Sugar Twists, 14
Cookie Dough
Cookie Dough Monkey Bread,
10
Cookie Sundae Cups, 150
Cookie Dough Monkey Bread, 10
Cookie Sundae Cups, 150
Corn
Chili Corn Bread, 116
Corn Chowder, 118
Corn Fritters, 114
Corn Chowder, 118
Corn Fritters, 114
Cream Cheese Cupcakes, 126
Crescent Dough: Cinnamon-
Sugar Twists, 14
Cupcakes
Banana Chocolate-Chunk
Cupcakes, 64
Cream Cheese Cupcakes, 126
Ice Cream Cone Cupcakes, 148
Leftover Candy Cupcakes with
Peanut Butter Frosting, 130
Curried Deviled Eggs, 58

D
Desserts
Banana Chocolate-Chunk
Cupcakes, 64
Cake Bonbons, 132
Chocolate Chip Cookie
Delights, 110
Chocolate-Covered Bacon, 46
Cinnamon-Sugar Twists, 14

Desserts *(continued)*
Cookie Sundae Cups, 150
Cream Cheese Cupcakes, 126
Frozen Chocolate-Covered
Bananas, 142
Ice Cream Cone Cupcakes,
148
Italian Cheesecake, 94
Leftover Candy Ice Cream
Sundae with Hard Chocolate
Topping, 138
Pumpkin Tartlets, 104
Wild Watermelon Pops, 146
Dinner
Not-So-Sloppy Joes, 140
Pumpkin Mac and Cheese, 80
Pumpkin Curry, 76
Pumpkin Ravioli, 74
Dipping Sauce, 92
Doughnuts
Mini Biscuit Doughnuts, 6
Quick Jelly-Filled Biscuit
Doughnuts, 8

E
Easy Cheesy Bacon Bread,
120
Easy Eggs Benedict, 54
Egg Salad Sandwiches, 56
Eggs
Bacon and Egg Cups, 42
Bacon and Egg Wraps, 52
Breakfast Flats, 36
Cheddar, Broccoli and
Mushroom Quiche, 50
Curried Deviled Eggs, 58
Easy Eggs Benedict, 54
Egg Salad Sandwiches, 56
Ham and Asparagus Quiche,
48
Huevos Ramencheros, 122
Ramen Egg Cups, 16

F
Focaccia with Rosemary and
  Romano, 96
Fruit
  Blueberry-Orange French
    Toast Casserole, 90
  Mixed Berry Dump Cake, 30
  Peach Strawberry Dump Cake,
    28
  Sweet and Savory Breakfast
    Muffins, 128

G
Ganache Frosting, 65

H
Ham and Asparagus Quiche, 48
Ham and Sausage
  Bacon and Egg Wraps, 52
  Easy Eggs Benedict, 54
  Ham and Asparagus Quiche,
    48
  Sausage and Kale Deep-Dish
    Mini Pizzas, 40
  Sweet and Savory Breakfast
    Muffins, 128
Huevos Ramencheros, 122

I
Ice Cream Cone Cupcakes, 148
Italian Cheesecake, 94
Italian Crouton Salad, 134

L
Leftover Candy Cupcakes with
  Peanut Butter Frosting, 130
Leftover Candy Ice Cream
  Sundae with Hard Chocolate
  Topping, 138
Lunch
  Corn Chowder, 118
  Egg Salad Sandwiches, 56
  Italian Crouton Salad, 134

Lunch (continued)
  Quick Waffled Quesadillas, 86
  Tahini Lentil Ramen Salad, 24
  Waffled Burger Sliders, 84

M
Mac and Cheese Mini Cups, 102
Macaroni and Cheese
  Mac and Cheese Mini Cups, 102
  No-Fuss Macaroni and Cheese,
    98
  Pumpkin Mac and Cheese, 80
  Ramen Bites on a Stick, 18
  Waffled Panko Mac and
    Cheese, 88
Meat Loaf Cupcakes, 144
Mini Biscuit Doughnuts, 6
Mini Fruit Coffeecakes, 106
Minty Cookies and Cream Cake,
  34
Mixed Berry Dump Cake, 30
Monkey Bread
  Cookie Dough Monkey Bread,
    10
  Easy Cheesy Bacon Bread, 120
  Pepperoni Pizza Monkey Bread,
    100
Muffin Tin
  Bacon and Egg Cups, 42
  Banana Chocolate-Chunk
    Cupcakes, 64
  Broccoli Surprise Corn Muffins,
    152
  Chocolate Chip Cookie
    Delights, 110
  Cookie Sundae Cups, 150
  Cream Cheese Cupcakes, 126
  Leftover Candy Cupcakes with
    Peanut Butter Frosting, 130
  Mac and Cheese Mini Cups, 102
  Meat Loaf Cupcakes, 144
  Mini Fruit Coffeecakes, 106
  Pepperoni Pizza Rolls, 38

Muffin Tin (continued)
Pepperoni Puffers, 22
Pumpkin Tartlets, 104
Quick and Easy Arancini, 108
Ramen Egg Cups, 16
Ripe Banana Muffins, 66
Sausage and Kale Deep-Dish
Mini Pizzas, 40
Sweet and Savory Breakfast
Muffins, 128
Tortilla Cups with Corn and
Black Bean Salad, 112
Mushrooms: Cheddar, Broccoli
and Mushroom Quiche, 50

N
No-Fuss Macaroni and Cheese,
98
Not-So-Sloppy Joes, 140
Nuts
Chocolate Chip-Banana Muffin
Bars, 60
Ripe Banana Muffins, 66
Tropical Turkey Salad, 136

P
Pasta
Mac and Cheese Mini Cups,
102
No-Fuss Macaroni and Cheese,
98
Pumpkin Mac and Cheese, 80
Sausage Spaghetti, 142
Waffled Panko Mac and
Cheese, 88
PB & J Sandwich Cake, 26
Peach Strawberry Dump Cake,
28
Peanut Butter
Leftover Candy Cupcakes with
Peanut Butter Frosting, 130
PB & J Sandwich Cake, 26

Pepperoni
Pepperoni Pizza Monkey Bread,
100
Pepperoni Pizza Rolls, 38
Pepperoni Puffers, 22
Pepperoni Pizza Monkey Bread,
100
Pepperoni Pizza Rolls, 38
Pepperoni Puffers, 22
Pizza Dough
Breakfast Flats, 36
Pepperoni Pizza Rolls, 38
Sausage and Kale Deep-Dish
Mini Pizzas, 40
Potatoes
Cheesy Mashed Potato Waffles,
82
Corn Chowder, 118
Meat Loaf Cupcakes, 144
Pumpkin and Parmesan Twice-
Baked Potatoes, 72
Puff Pastry: Mini Fruit
Coffeecakes, 106
Pumpkin
Pumpkin and Parmesan Twice-
Baked Potatoes, 72
Pumpkin Curry, 76
Pumpkin Mac and Cheese,
80
Pumpkin Ravioli, 74
Pumpkin Spice Latte, 78
Pumpkin Tartlets, 104
Pumpkin and Parmesan Twice-
Baked Potatoes, 72
Pumpkin Curry, 76
Pumpkin Mac and Cheese,
80
Pumpkin Ravioli, 74
Pumpkin Spice Latte, 78
Pumpkin Tartlets, 104

Q
Quick and Easy Arancini, 108
Quick Jelly-Filled Biscuit
      Doughnuts, 8
Quick Waffled Quesadillas, 86

R
Rainbow Cake, 32
Ramen Bites on a Stick, 18
Ramen Egg Cups, 16
Ramen French Toast, 20
Ramen Noodles
      Huevos Ramencheros, 122
      Pepperoni Puffers, 22
      Ramen Bites on a Stick, 18
      Ramen Egg Cups, 16
      Ramen French Toast, 20
      Tahini Lentil Ramen Salad, 24
Rice
      Pumpkin Curry, 76
      Quick and Easy Arancini, 108
Ripe Banana Muffins, 66

S
Sausage and Kale Deep-Dish Mini
      Pizzas, 40
Sausage Spaghetti, 142
Snacks
      Broccoli Surprise Corn Muffins,
      152
      Buttermilk Drop Biscuits,
      124
      Cheesy Mashed Potato Waffles,
      82
      Chocolate-Covered Bacon, 46
      Cookie Dough Monkey Bread,
      10
      Curried Deviled Eggs, 58
      Focaccia with Rosemary and
      Romano, 96
      Mac and Cheese Mini Cups,
      102

Snacks *(continued)*
      Pepperoni Pizza Monkey Bread,
      100
      Pepperoni Puffers, 22
      Quick Waffled Quesadillas,
      86
      Ramen Bites on a Stick, 18
      Tortilla Cups with Corn and
      Black Bean Salad, 112
      Waffled Burger Sliders, 84
      Wild Watermelon Pops, 146
Spiced Banana Bread, 62
Spiced Maple Banana Oatmeal
      Smoothie, 68
Steamed Pork Buns, 92
Super Simple Cheesy Bubble
      Loaf, 12
Sweet and Savory Breakfast
      Muffins, 128

T
Tahini Lentil Ramen Salad, 24
Tofu: Pumpkin Curry, 76
Tortilla Cups with Corn and Black
      Bean Salad, 112
Tropical Turkey Salad, 136
Turkey: Tropical Turkey Salad,
      136

W
Waffled Burger Sliders, 84
Waffled Panko Mac and Cheese,
      88
Wild Watermelon Pops, 146

VOLUME MEASUREMENTS (dry)

$1/8$ teaspoon = 0.5 mL
$1/4$ teaspoon = 1 mL
$1/2$ teaspoon = 2 mL
$3/4$ teaspoon = 4 mL
1 teaspoon = 5 mL
1 tablespoon = 15 mL
2 tablespoons = 30 mL
$1/4$ cup = 60 mL
$1/3$ cup = 75 mL
$1/2$ cup = 125 mL
$2/3$ cup = 150 mL
$3/4$ cup = 175 mL
1 cup = 250 mL
2 cups = 1 pint = 500 mL
3 cups = 750 mL
4 cups = 1 quart = 1 L

VOLUME MEASUREMENTS (fluid)

1 fluid ounce (2 tablespoons) = 30 mL
4 fluid ounces ($1/2$ cup) = 125 mL
8 fluid ounces (1 cup) = 250 mL
12 fluid ounces ($1 1/2$ cups) = 375 mL
16 fluid ounces (2 cups) = 500 mL

WEIGHTS (mass)

$1/2$ ounce = 15 g
1 ounce = 30 g
3 ounces = 90 g
4 ounces = 120 g
8 ounces = 225 g
10 ounces = 285 g
12 ounces = 360 g
16 ounces = 1 pound = 450 g

DIMENSIONS

$1/16$ inch = 2 mm
$1/8$ inch = 3 mm
$1/4$ inch = 6 mm
$1/2$ inch = 1.5 cm
$3/4$ inch = 2 cm
1 inch = 2.5 cm

OVEN TEMPERATURES

250°F = 120°C
275°F = 140°C
300°F = 150°C
325°F = 160°C
350°F = 180°C
375°F = 190°C
400°F = 200°C
425°F = 220°C
450°F = 230°C

BAKING PAN SIZES

Utensil	Size in Inches/Quarts	Metric Volume	Size in Centimeters
Baking or	$8\times8\times2$	2 L	$20\times20\times5$
Cake Pan	$9\times9\times2$	2.5 L	$23\times23\times5$
(square or	$12\times8\times2$	3 L	$30\times20\times5$
rectangular)	$13\times9\times2$	3.5 L	$33\times23\times5$
Loaf Pan	$8\times4\times3$	1.5 L	$20\times10\times7$
	$9\times5\times3$	2 L	$23\times13\times7$
Round Layer	$8\times1 1/2$	1.2 L	20×4
Cake Pan	$9\times1 1/2$	1.5 L	23×4
Pie Plate	$8\times1 1/4$	750 mL	20×3
	$9\times1 1/4$	1 L	23×3
Baking Dish	1 quart	1 L	—
or Casserole	$1 1/2$ quart	1.5 L	—
	2 quart	2 L	—